I express gratitude to God for all the blessings, My family is the essence of my existence.
Love you.

Talita Caires
2024

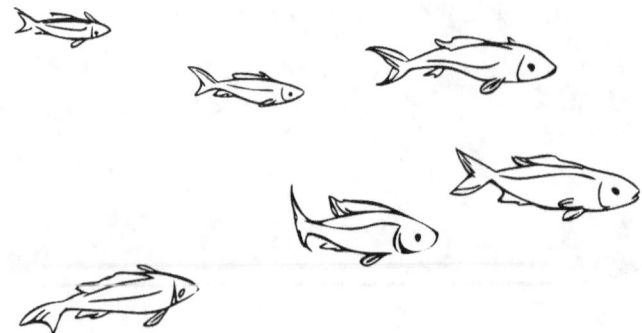

# This book belongs to:

○────────────────────────○

Talita Caires

## Talita Caires

# Test color page

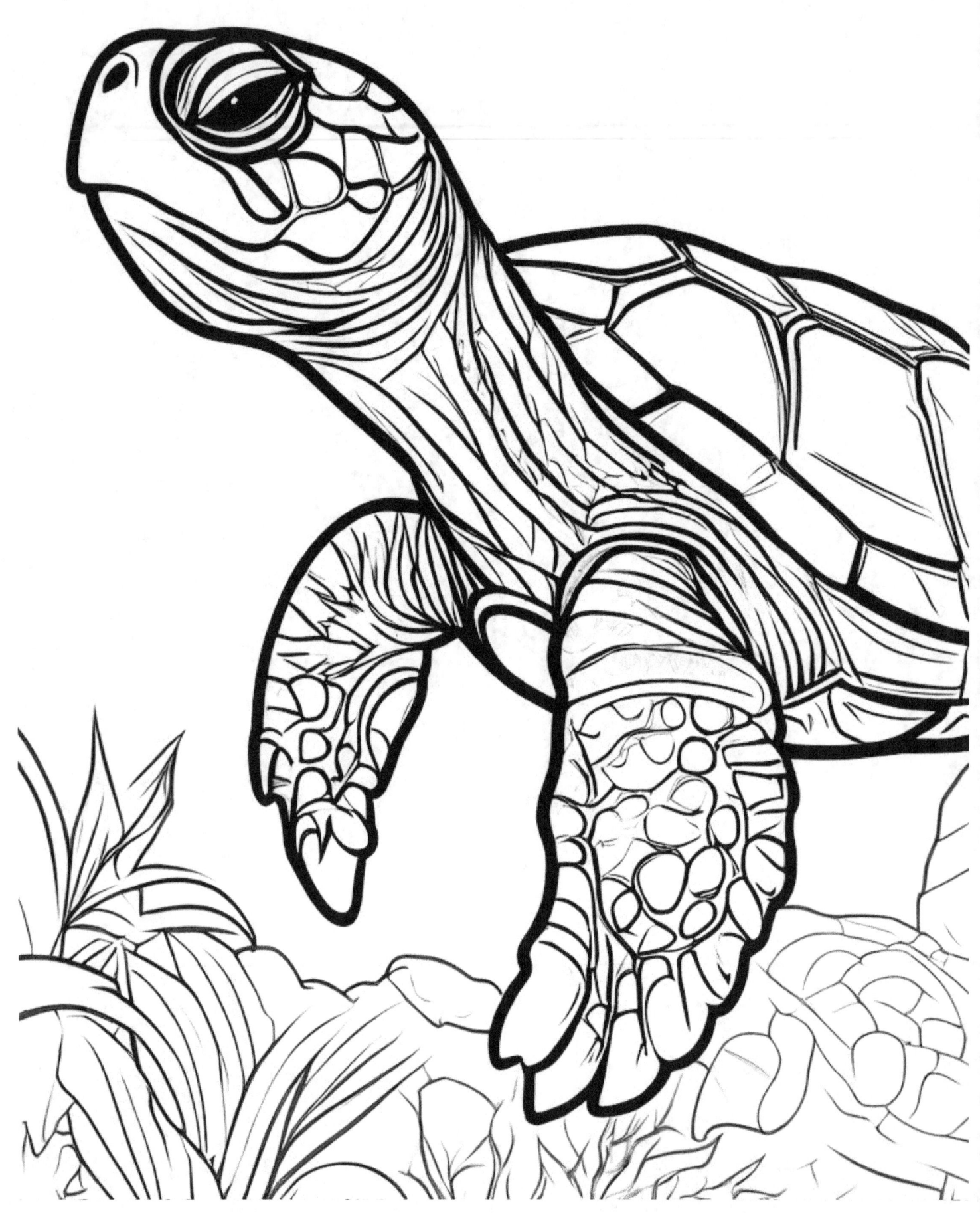

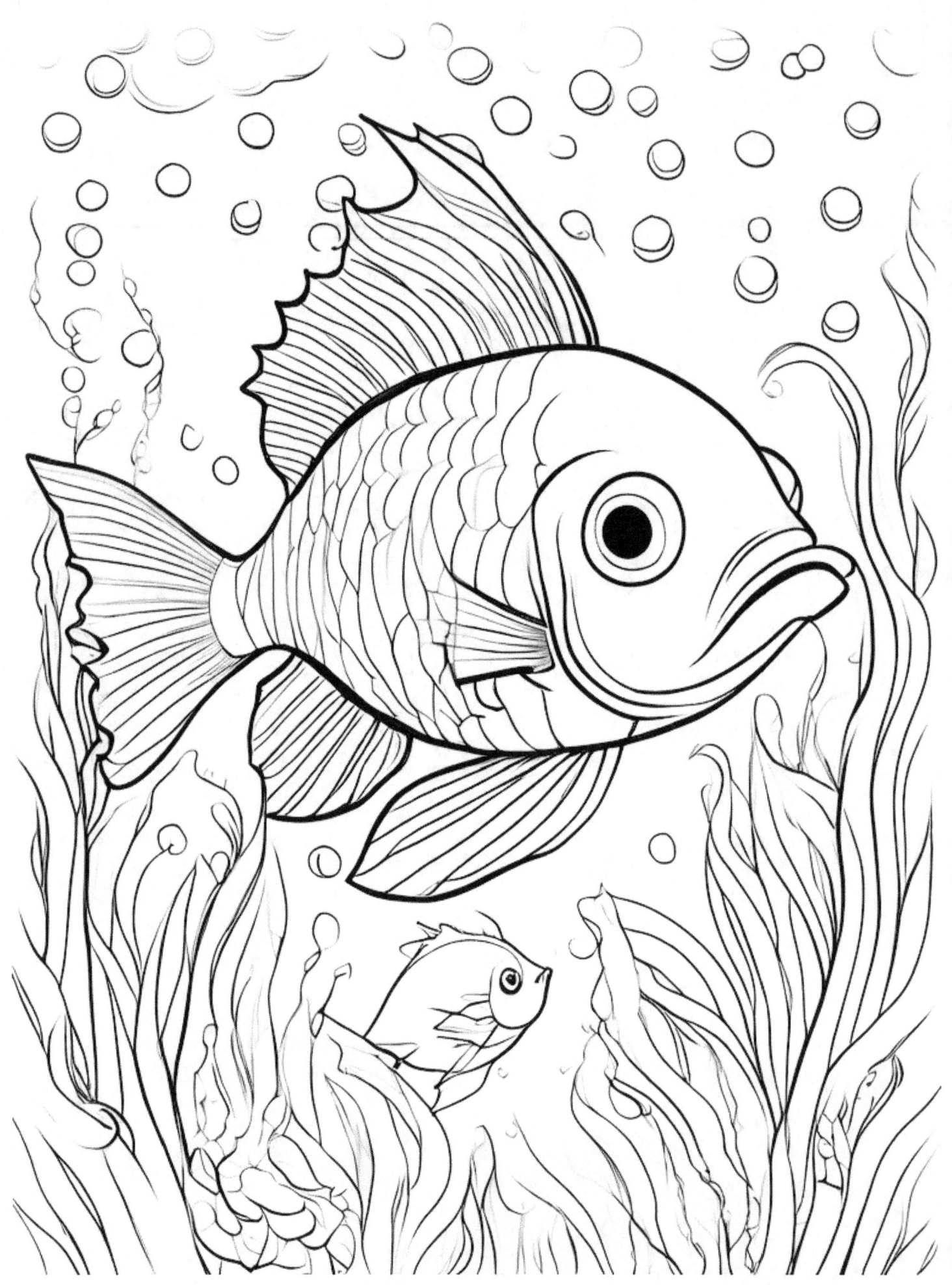

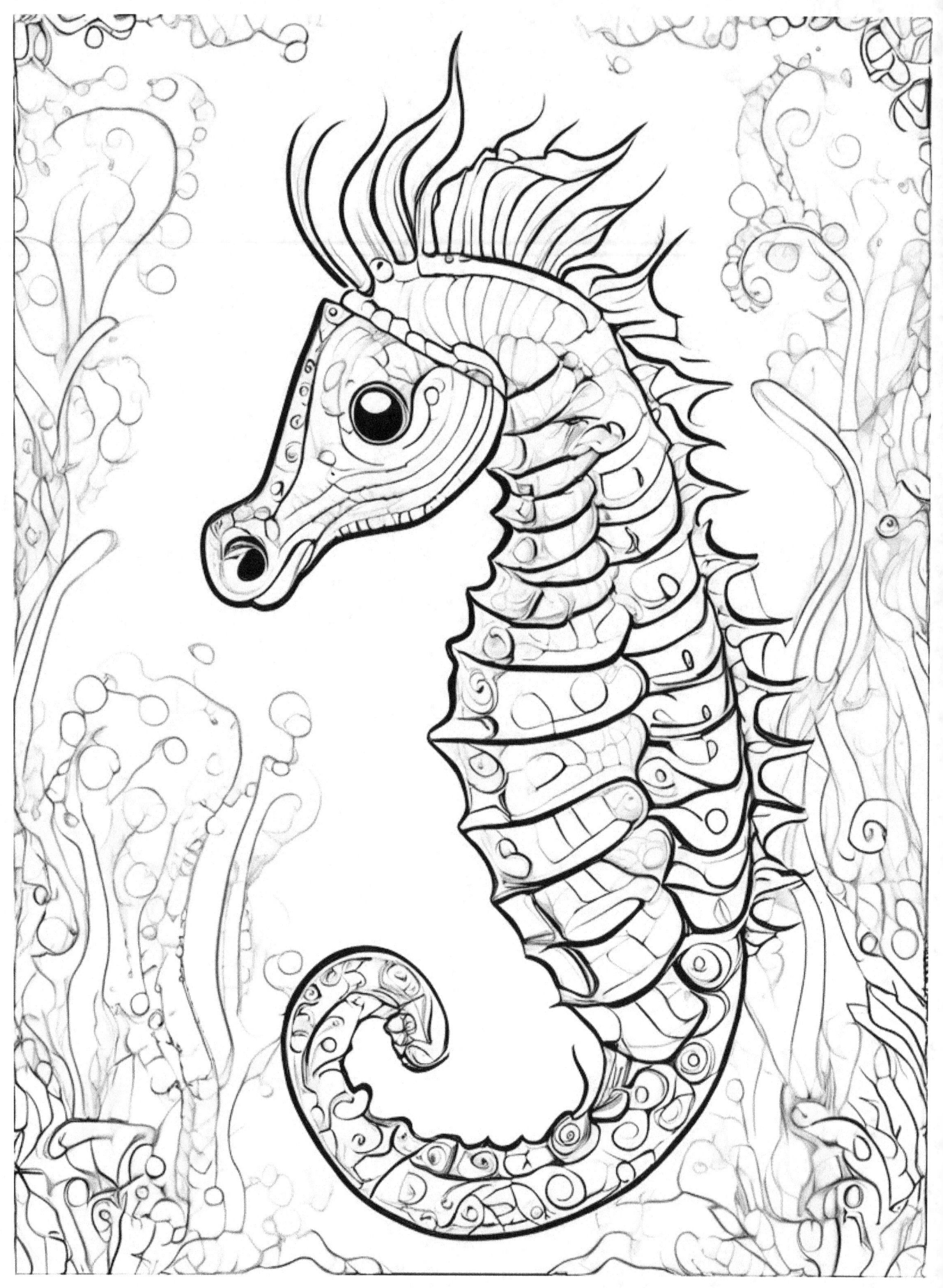

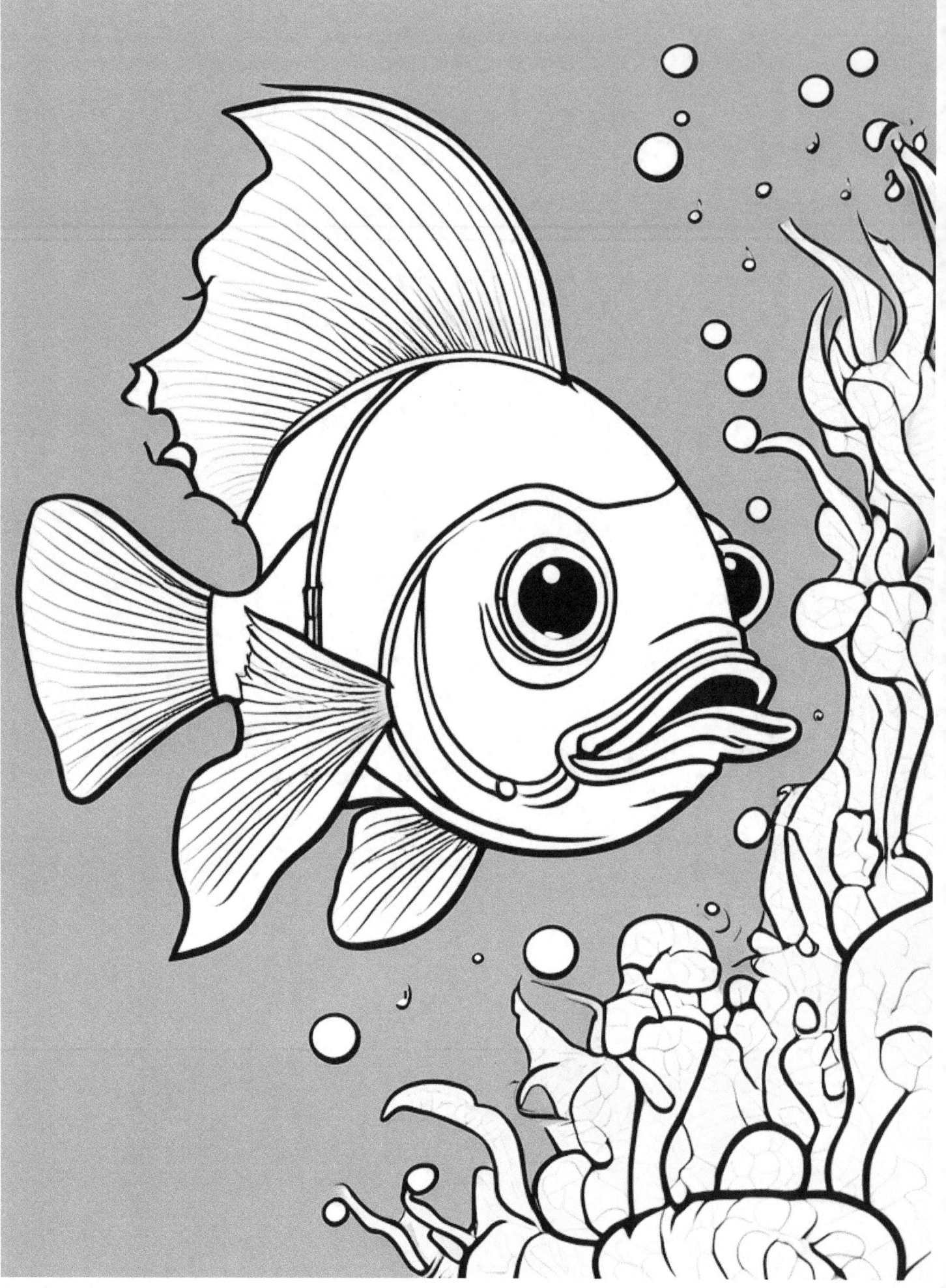

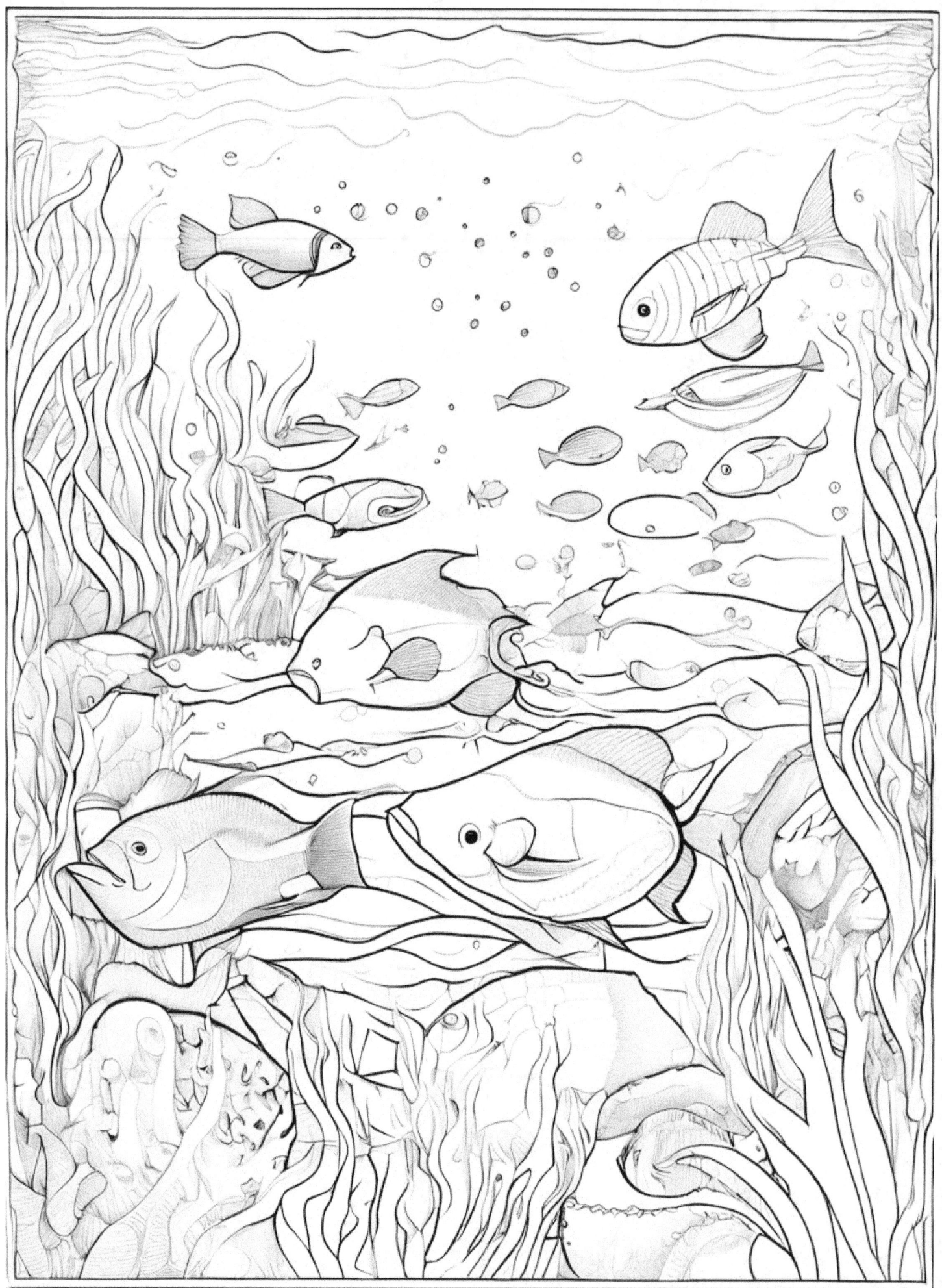

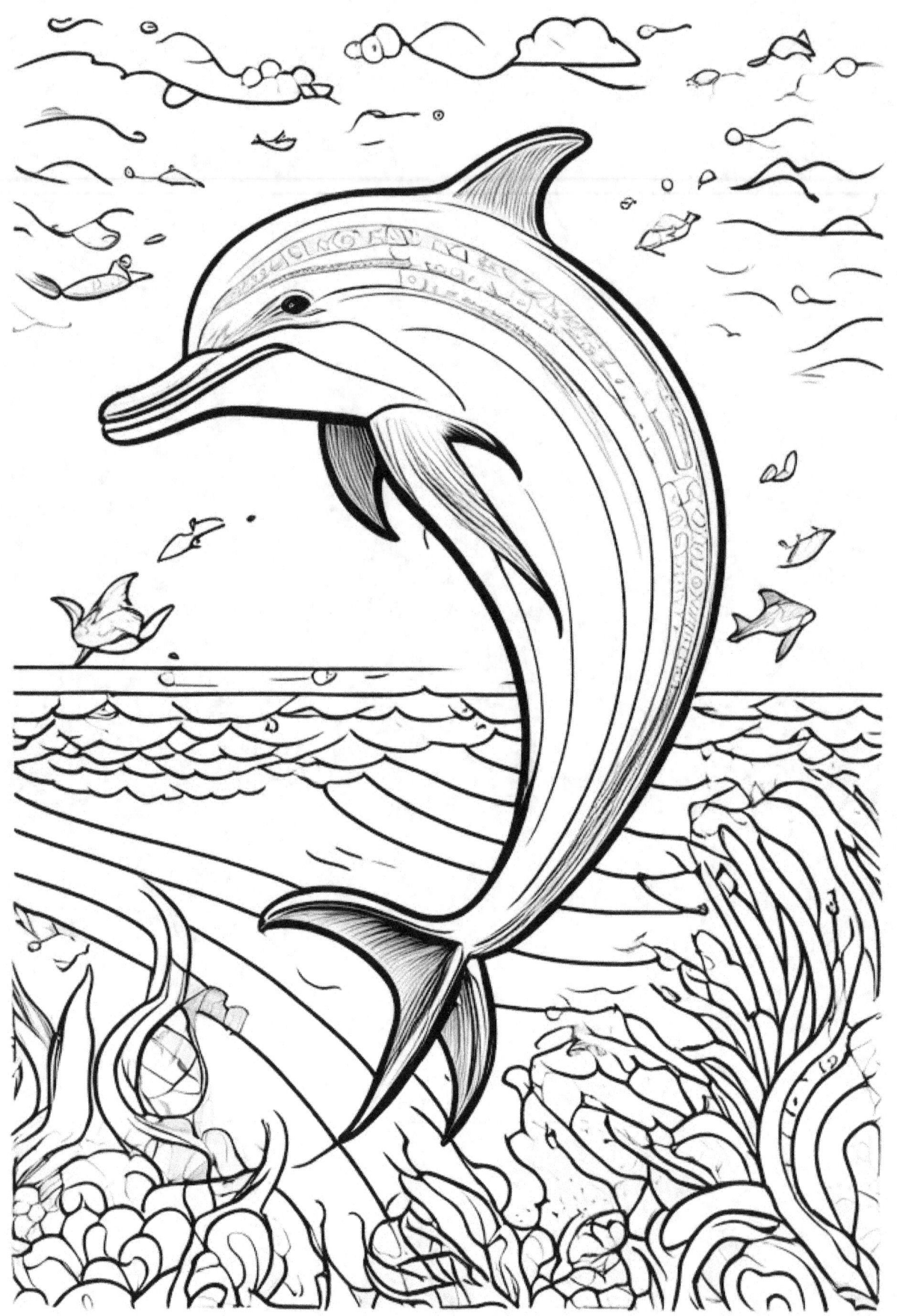

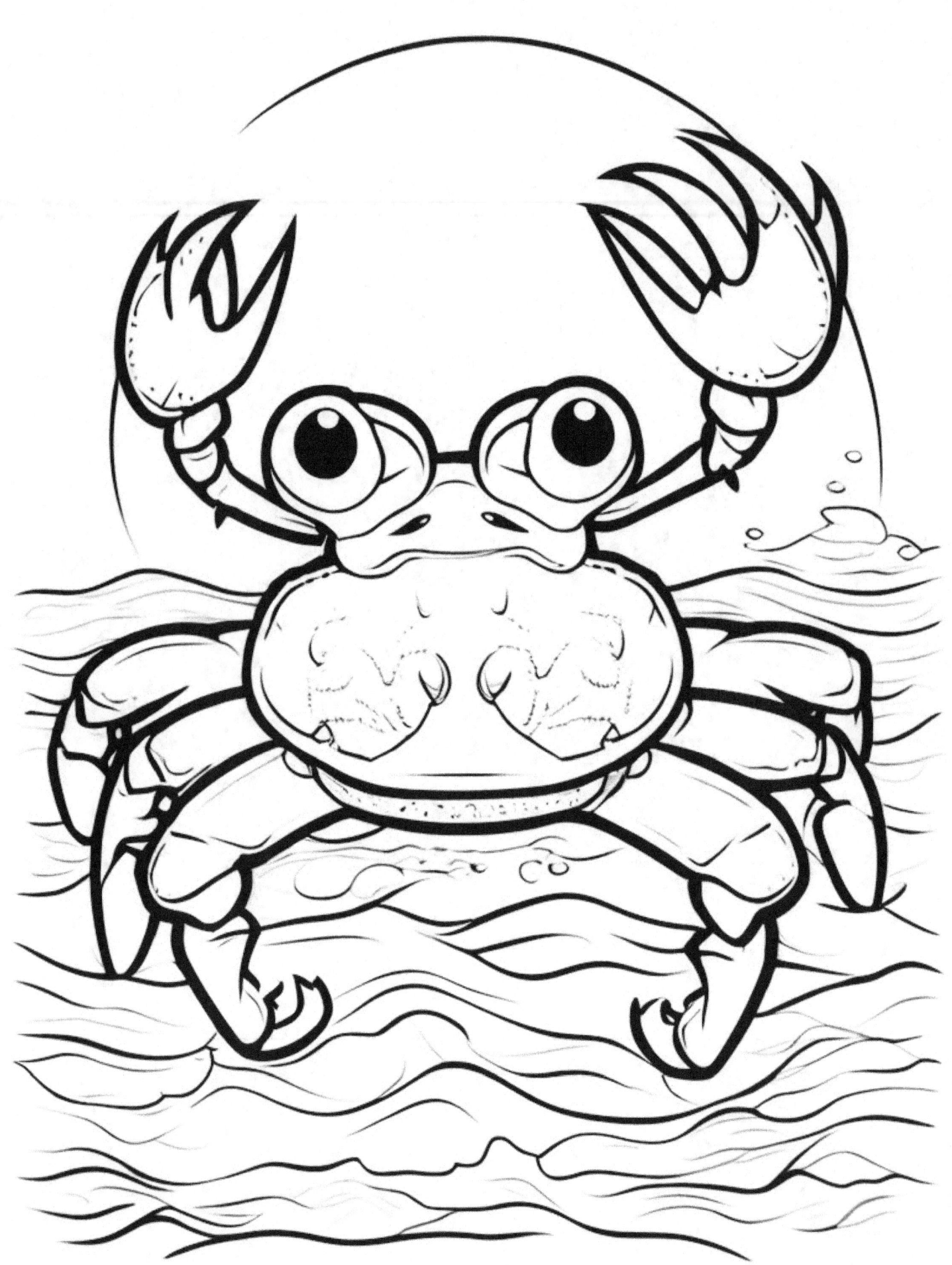

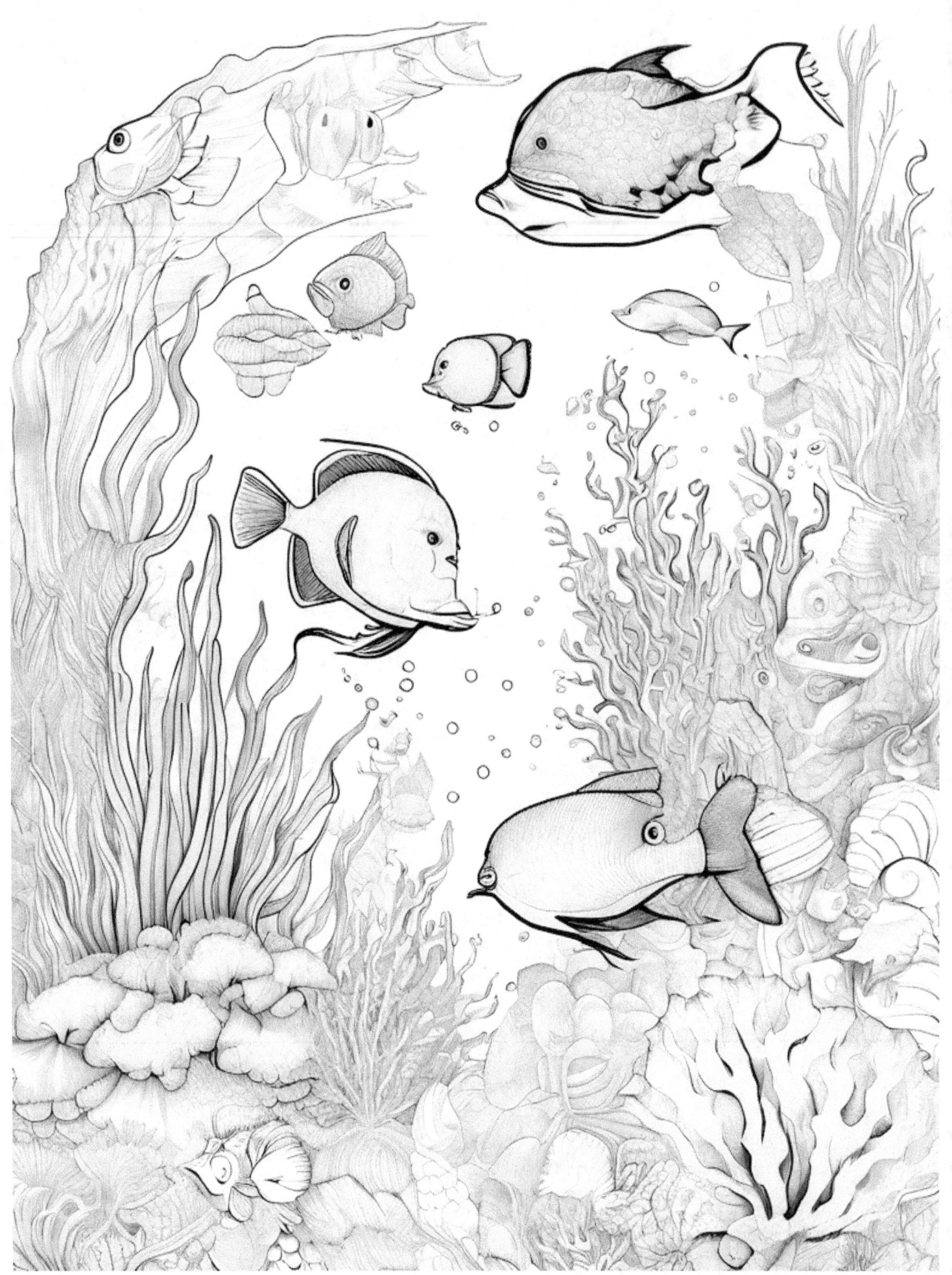

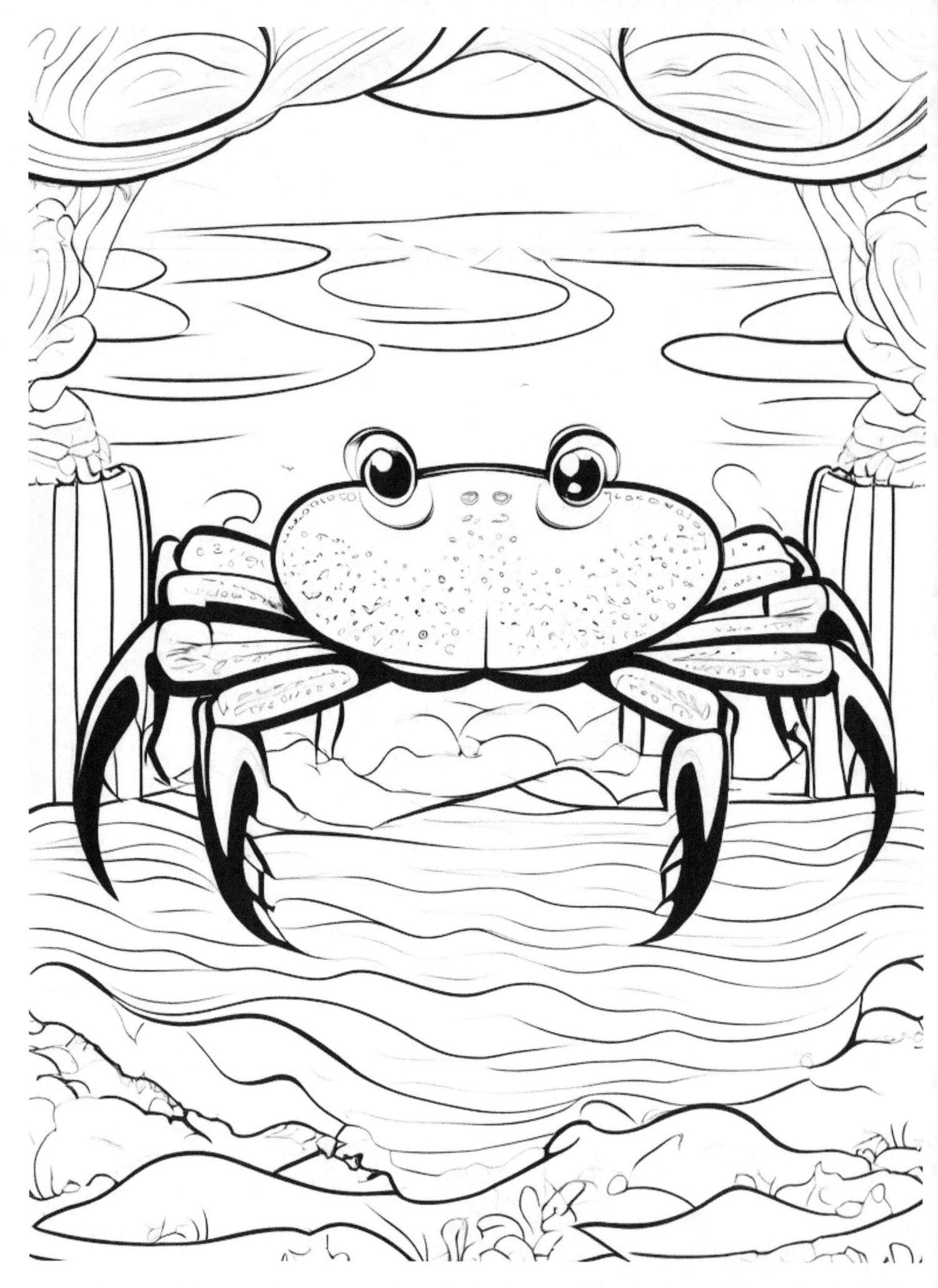

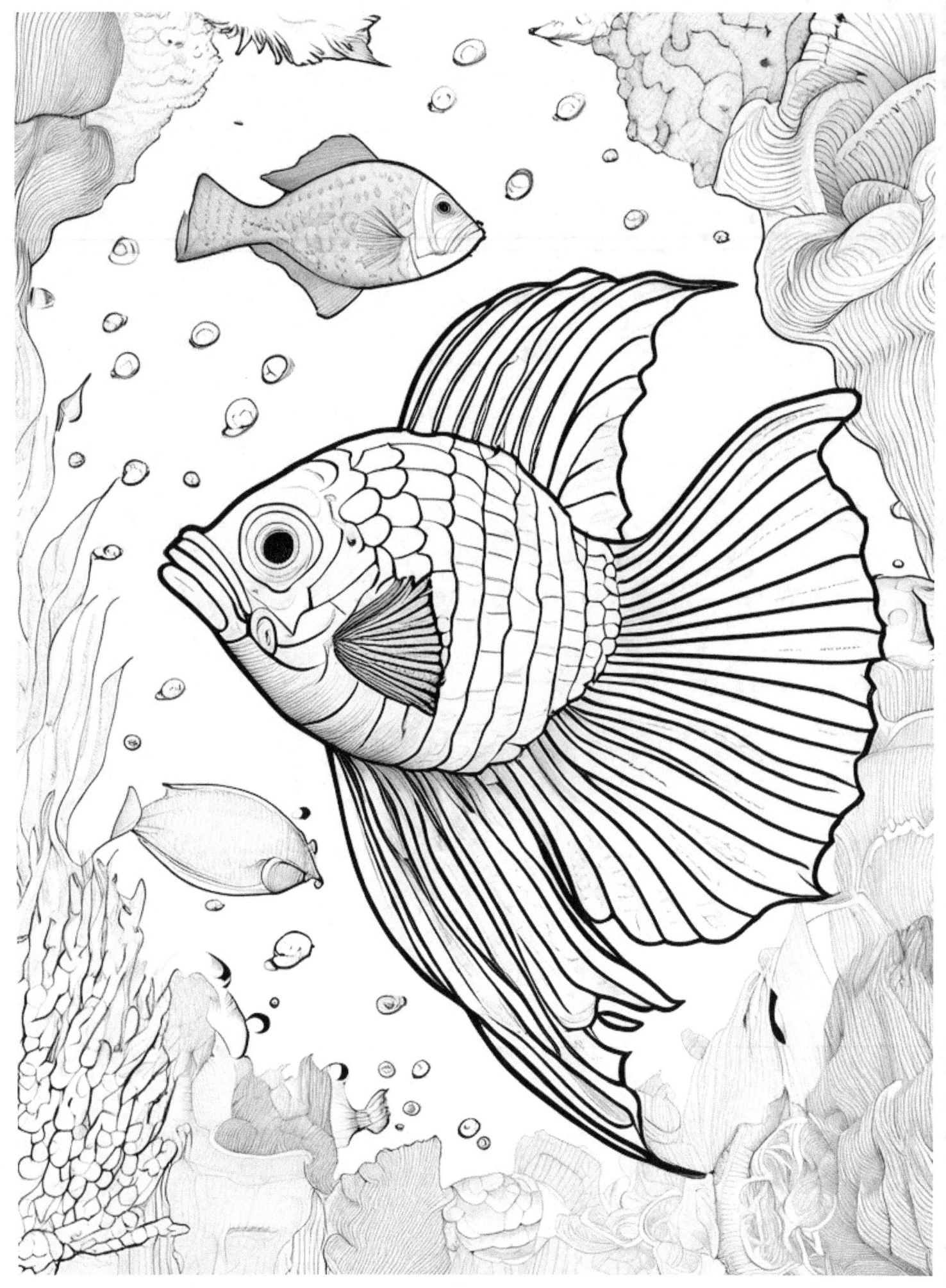

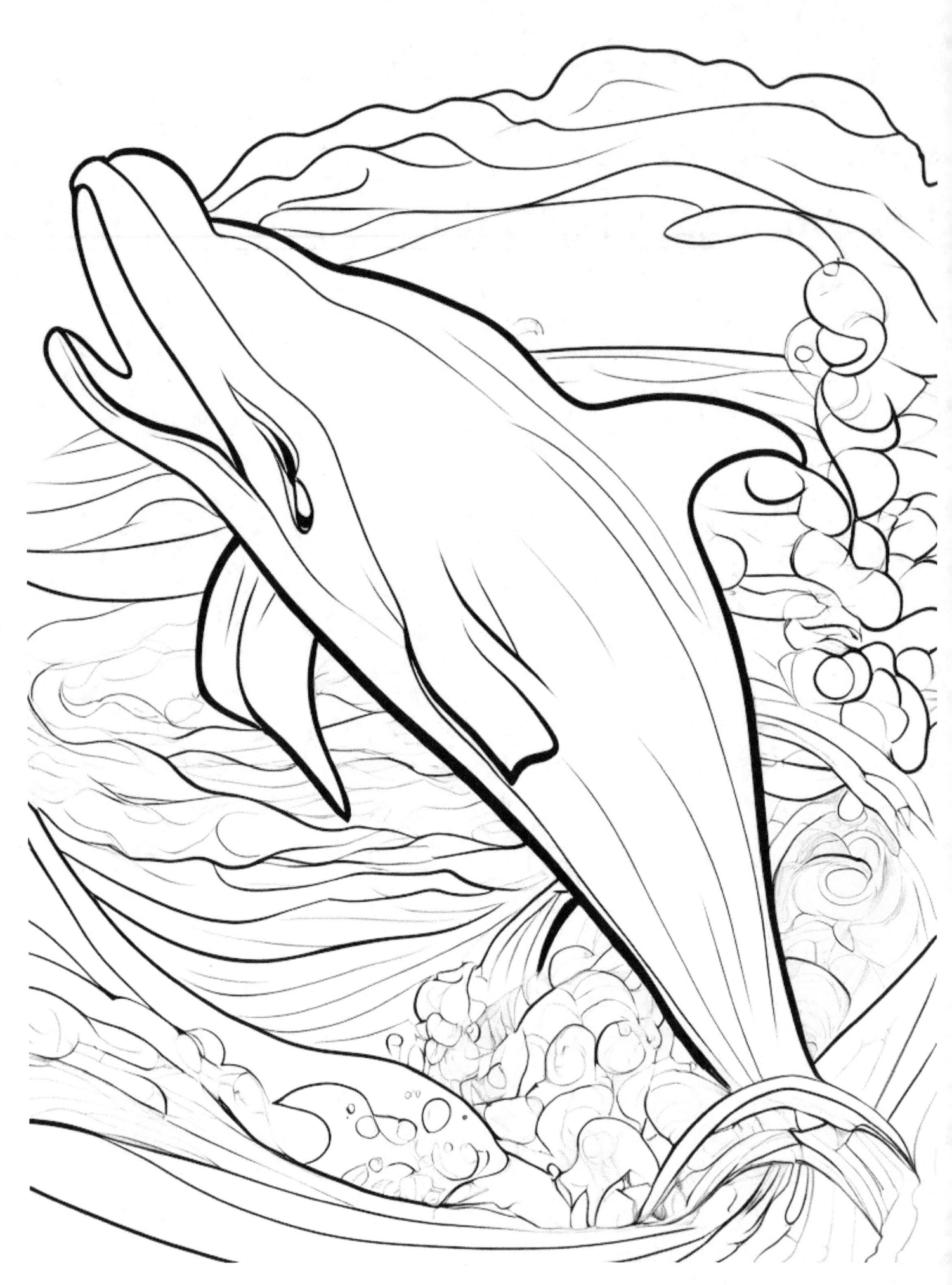

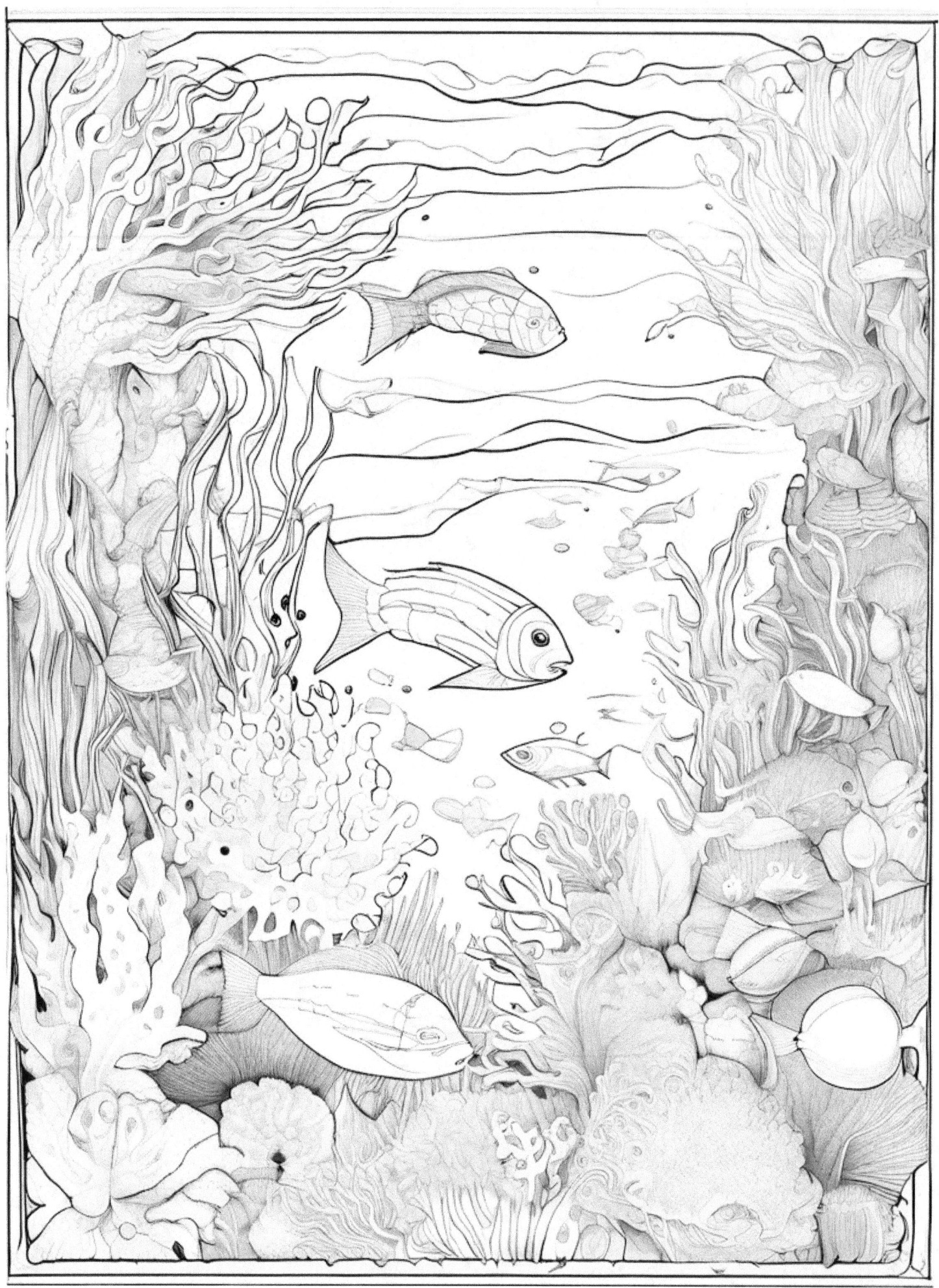

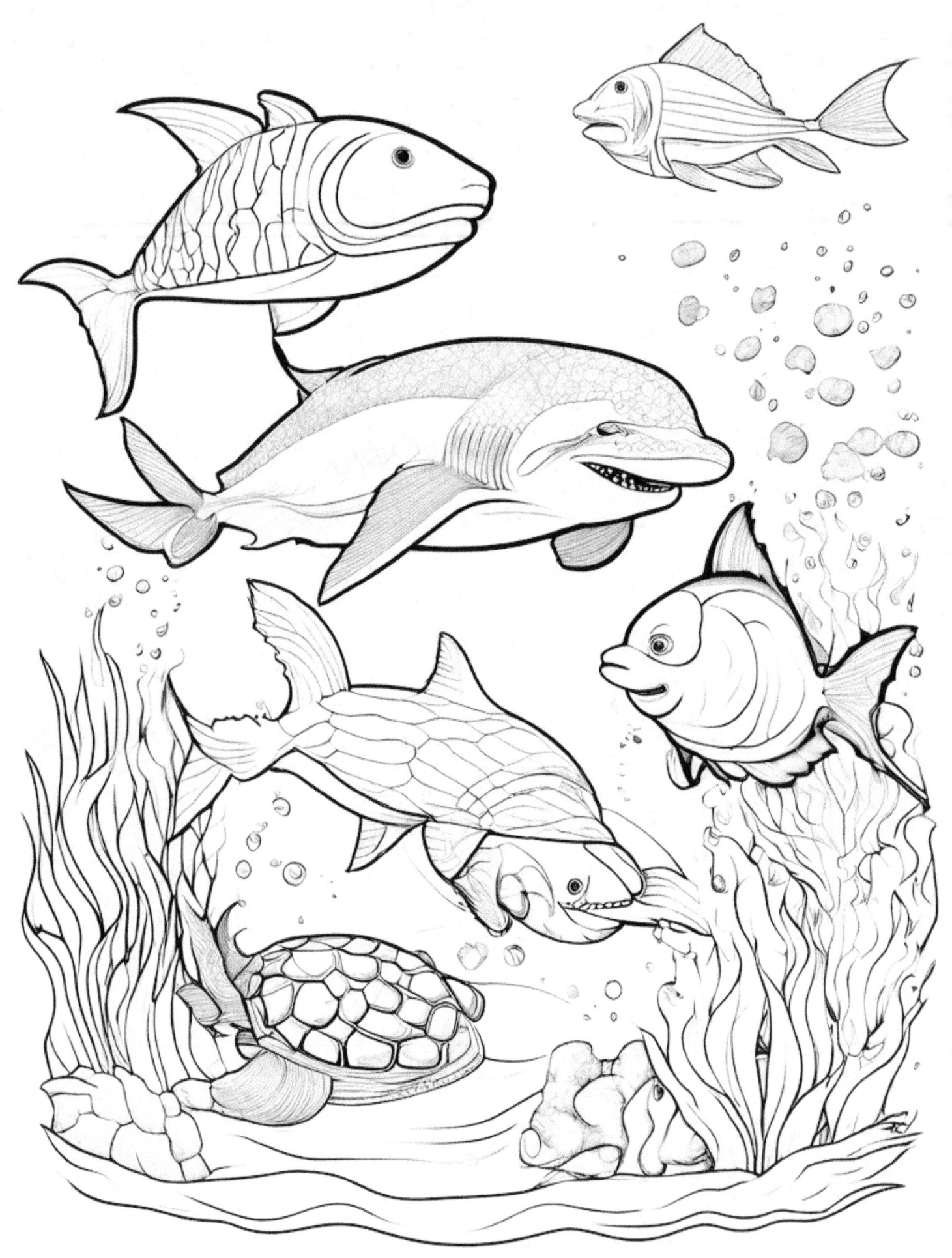

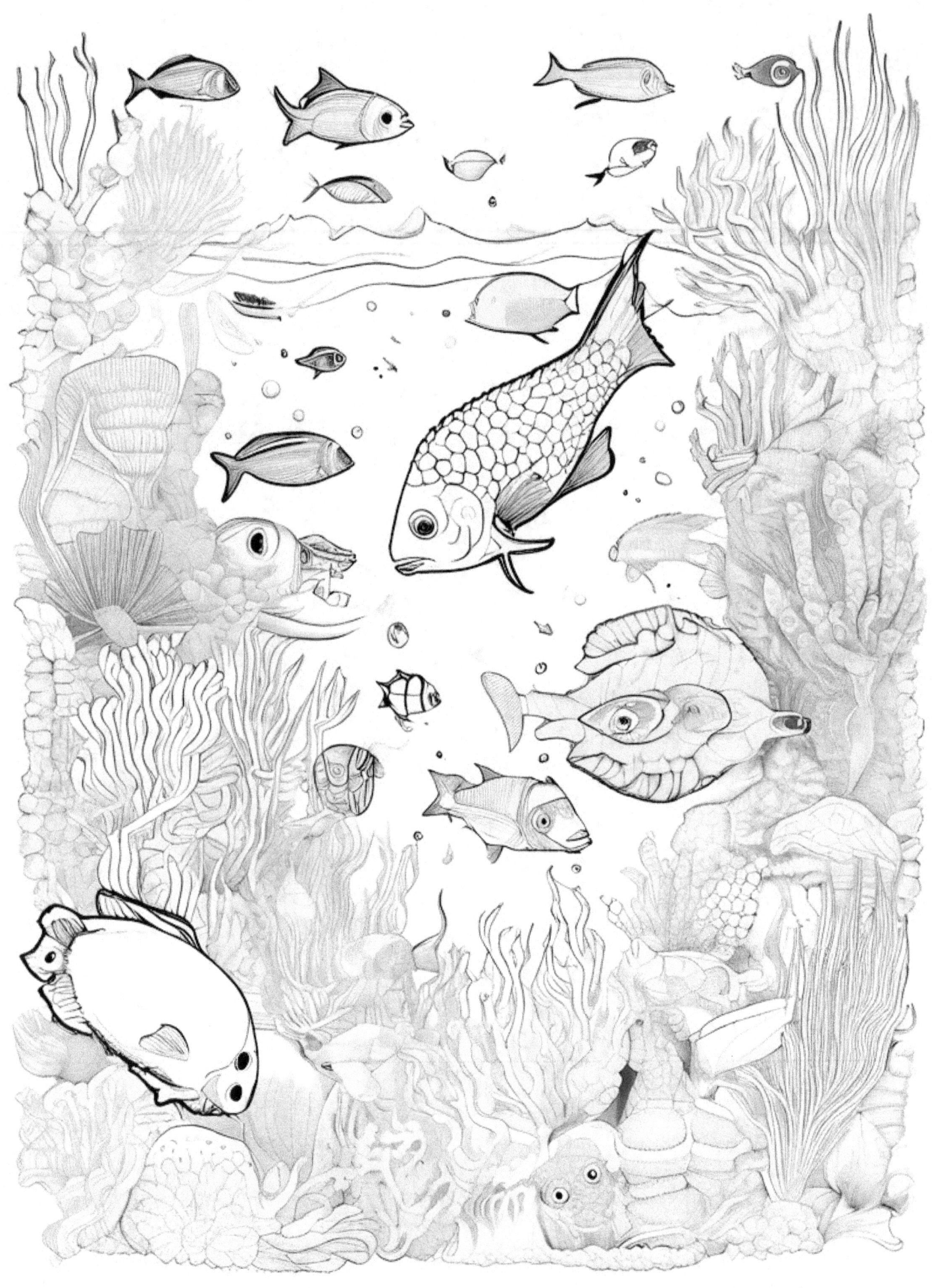

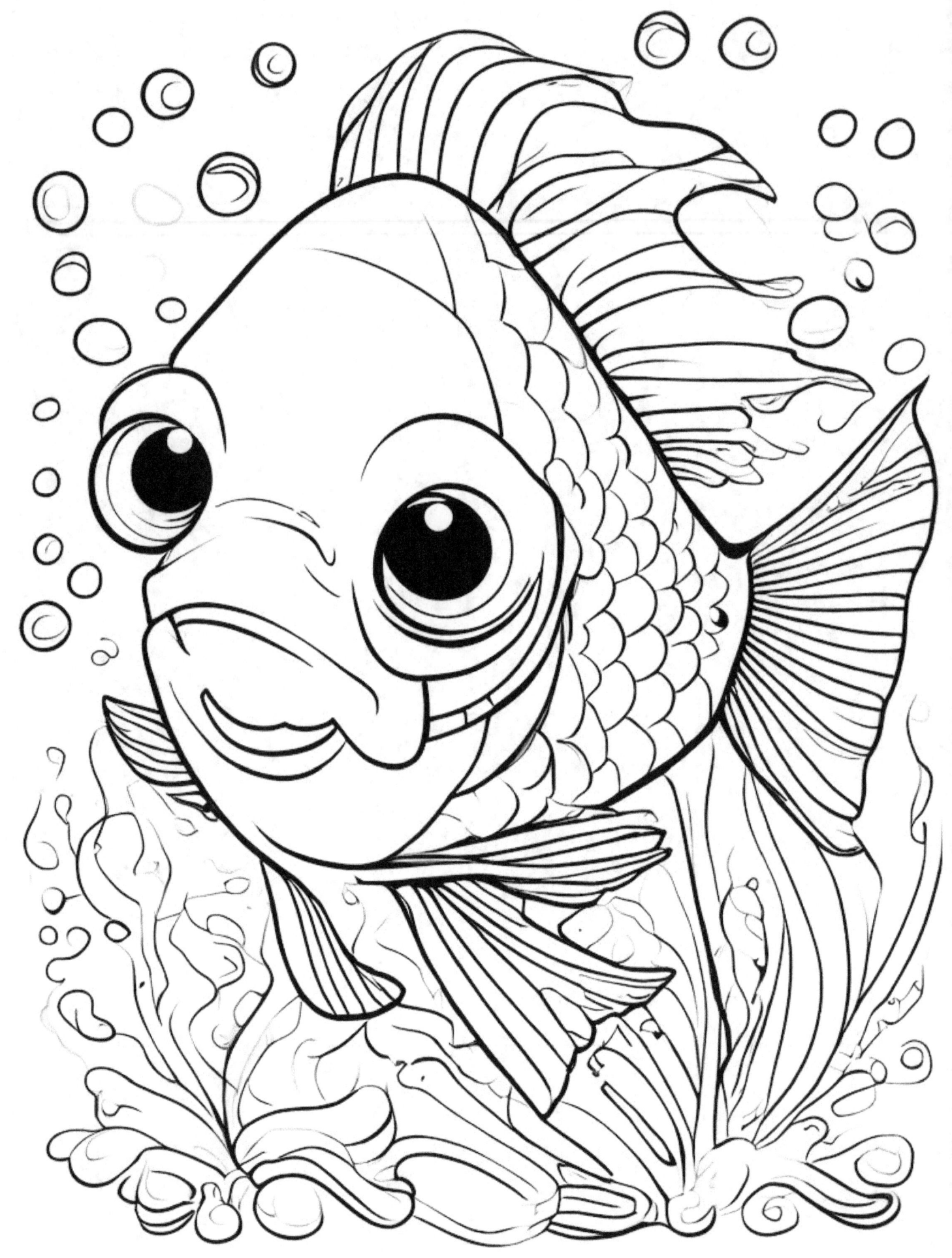

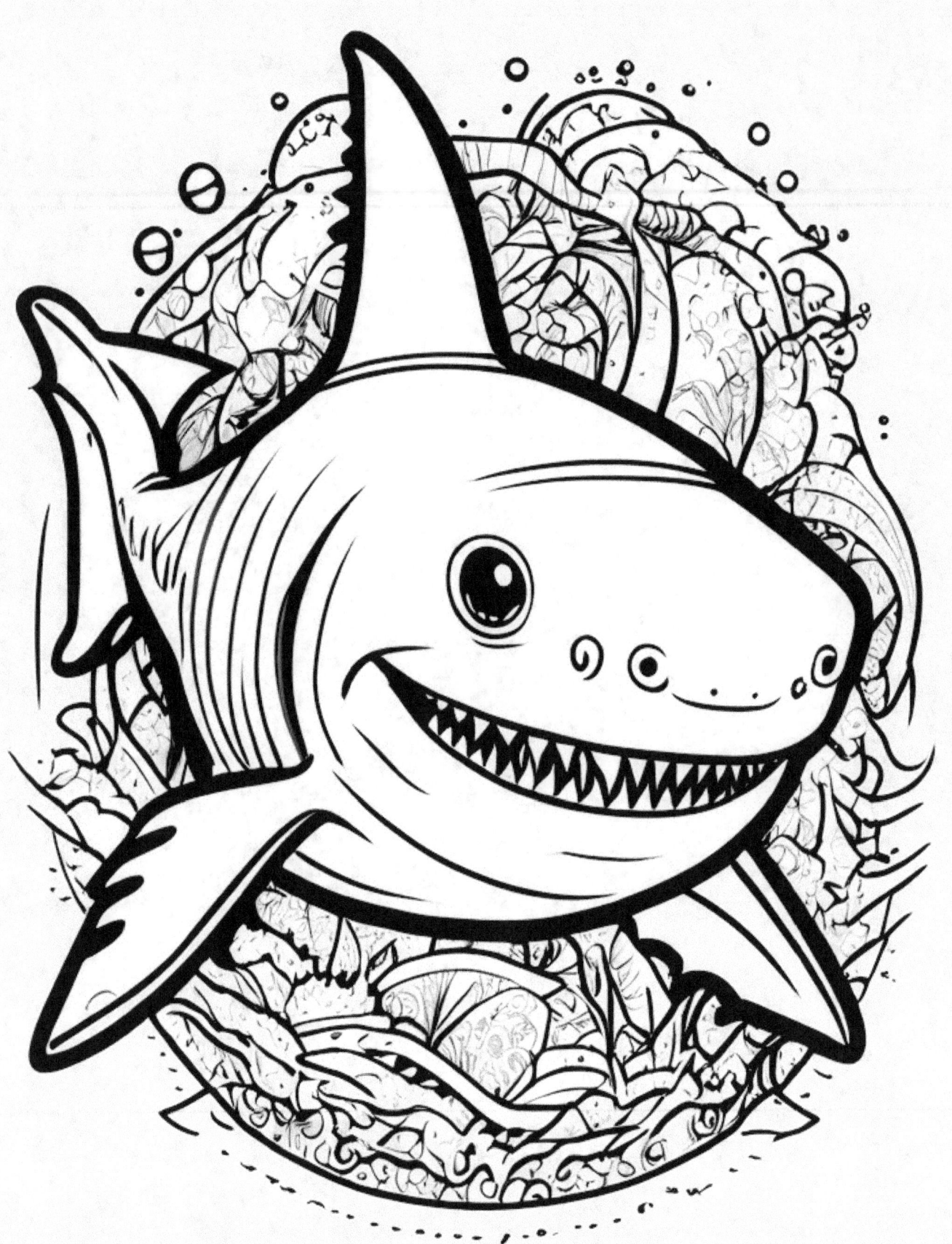

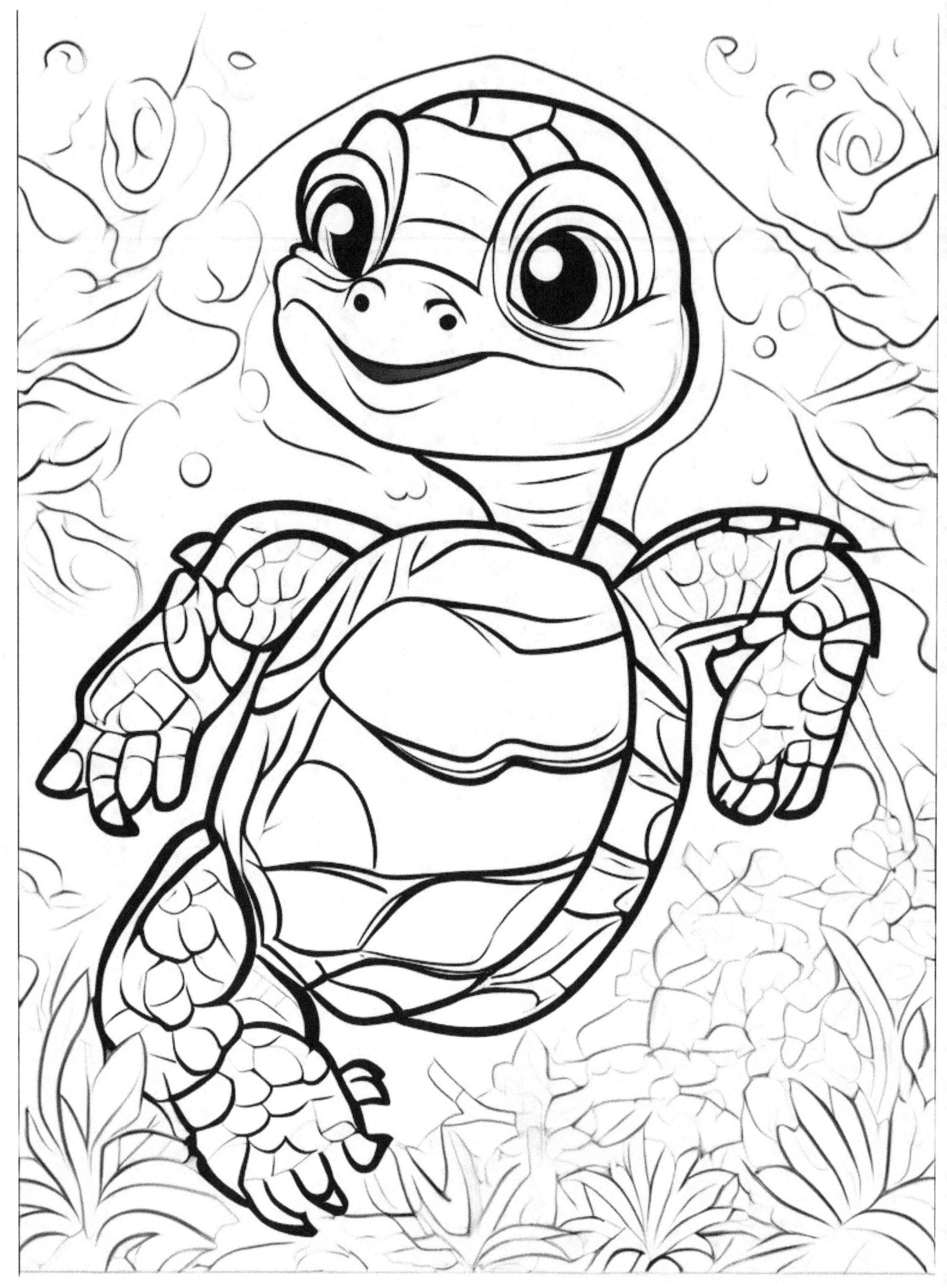

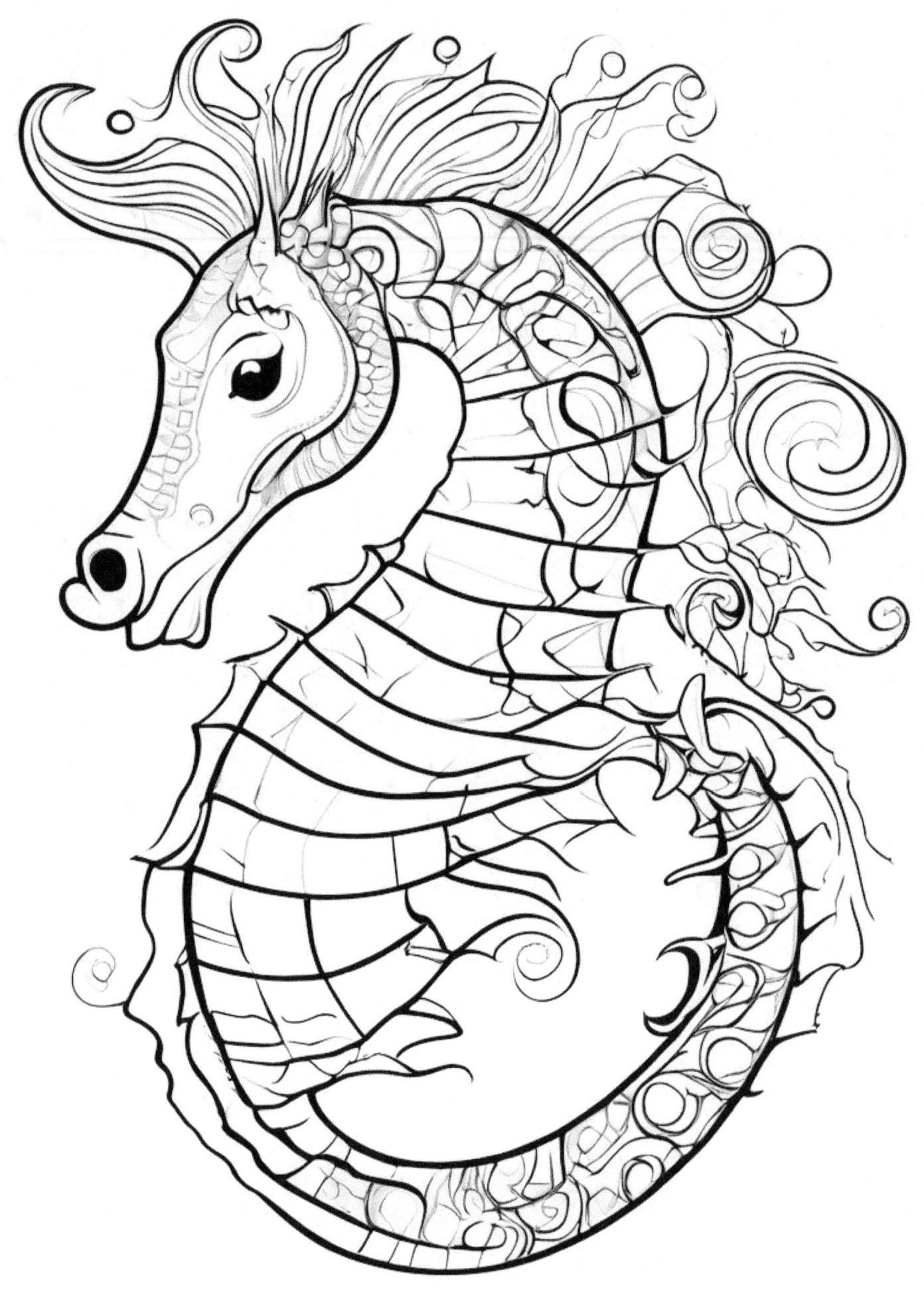

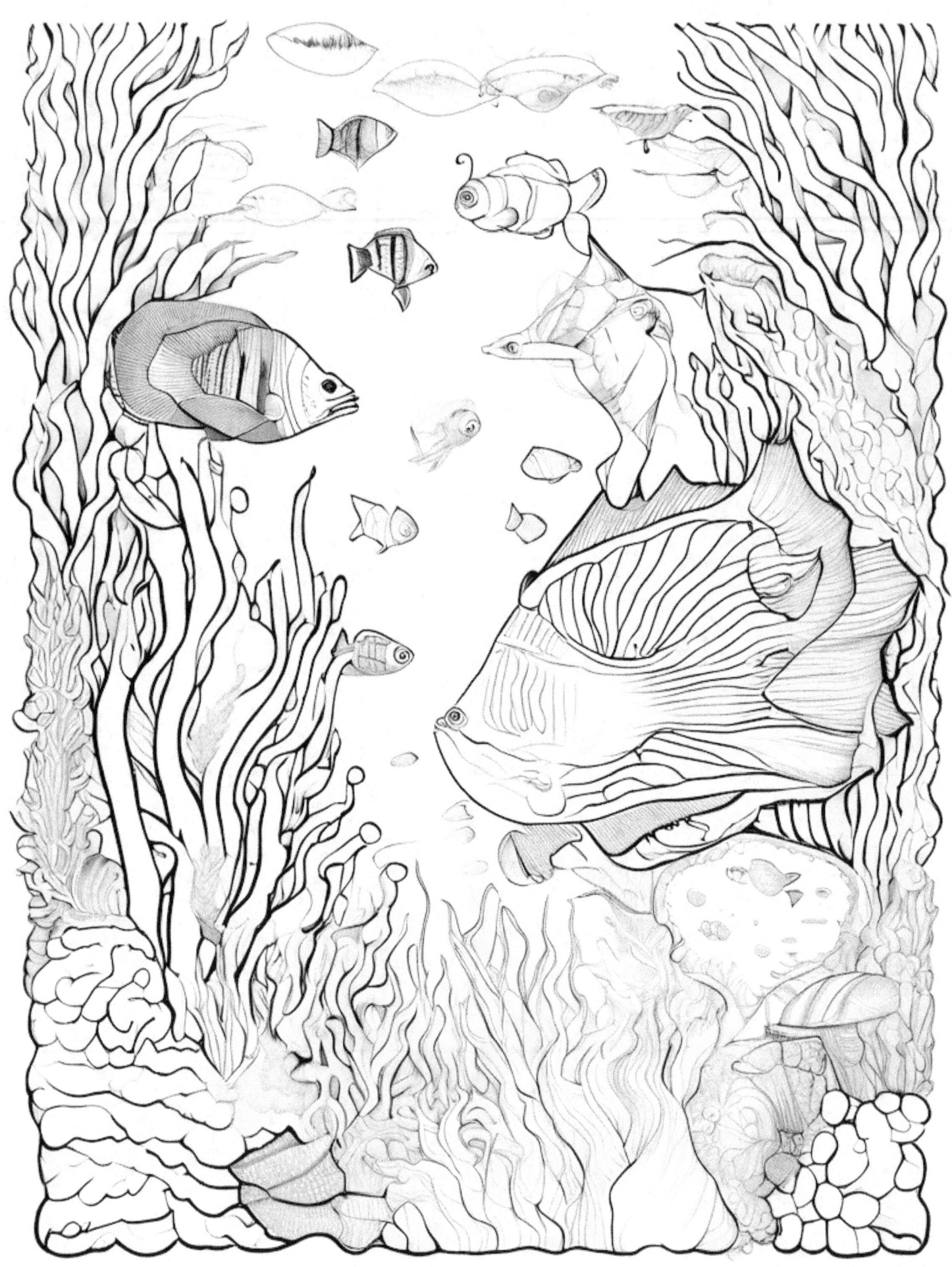

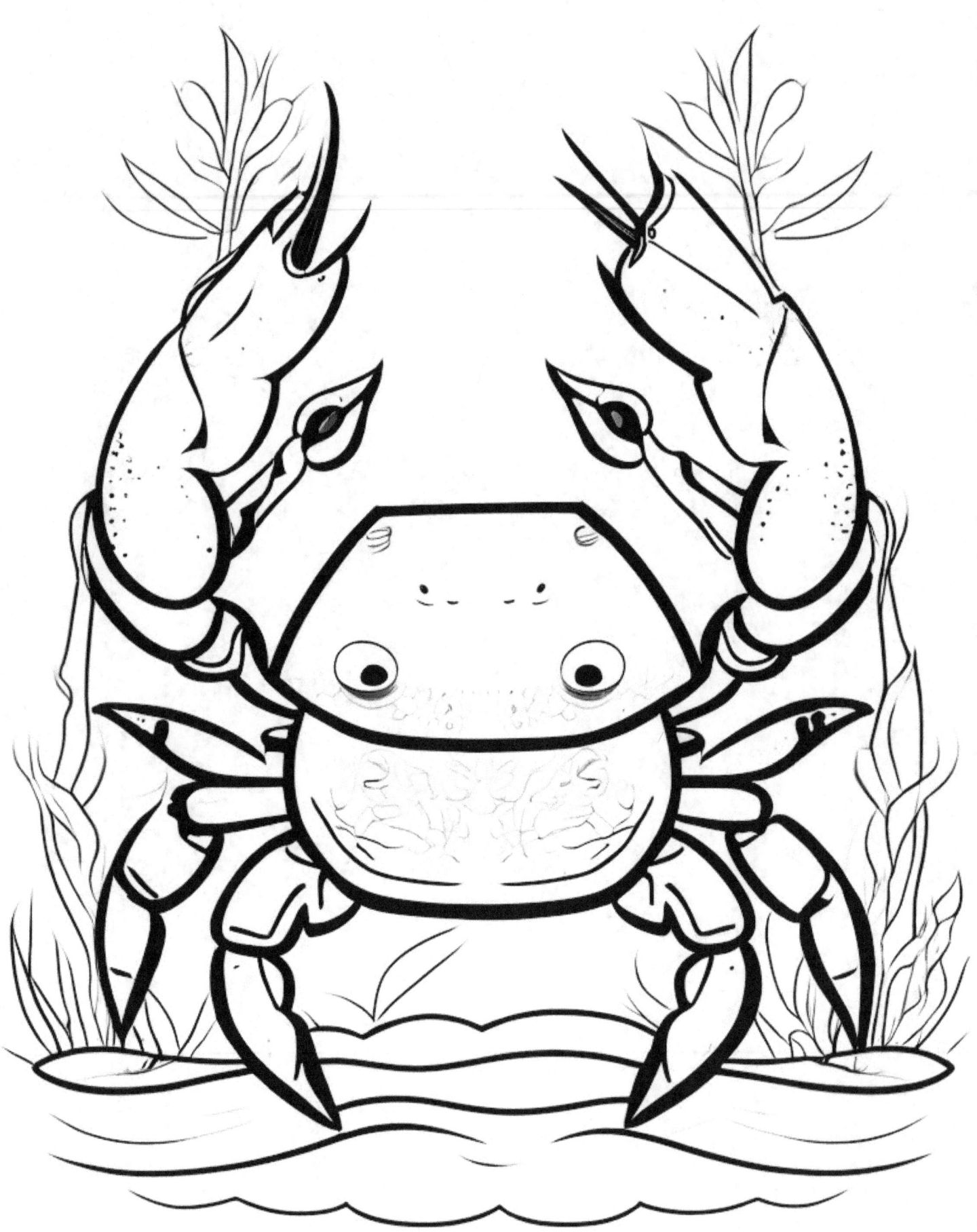

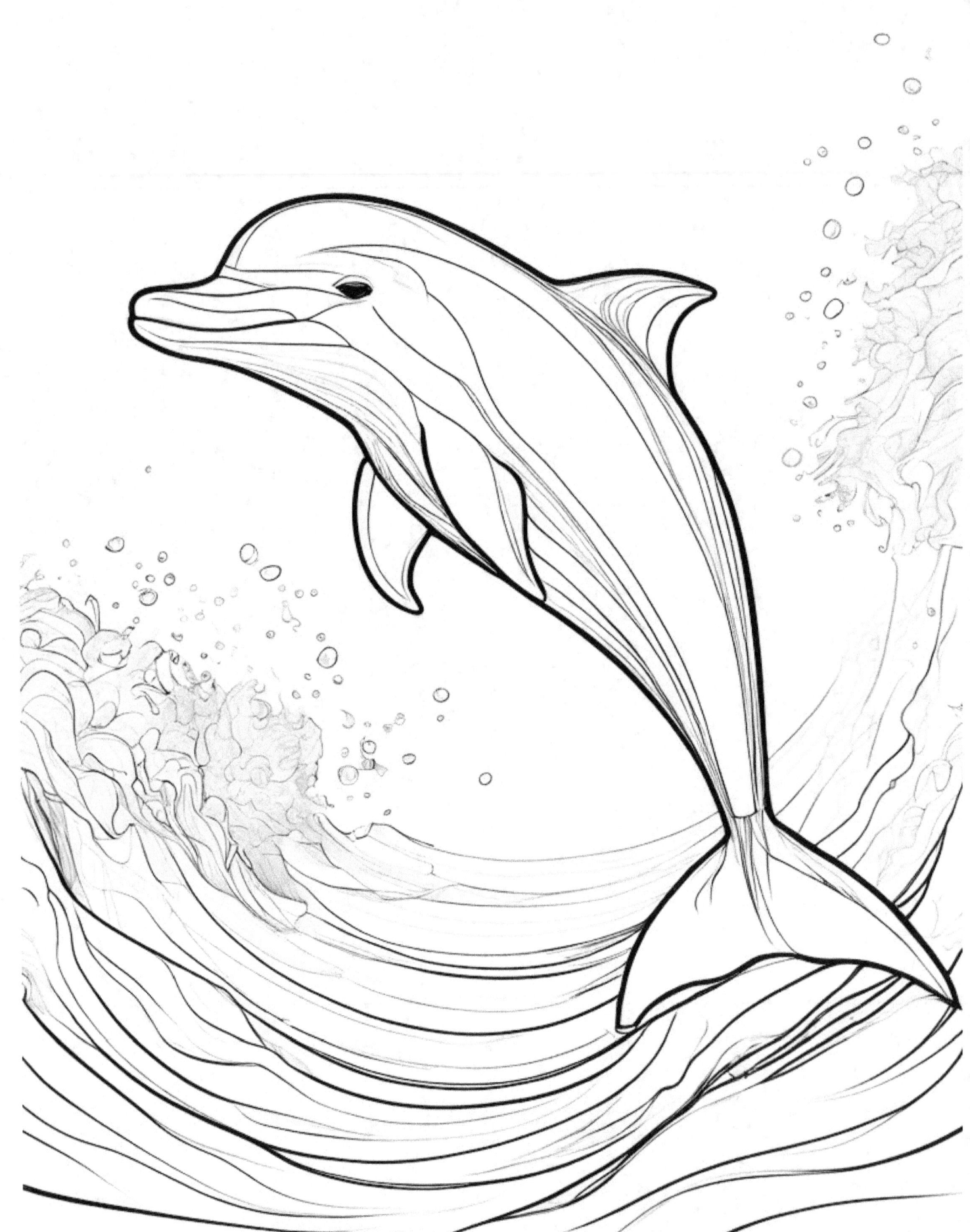

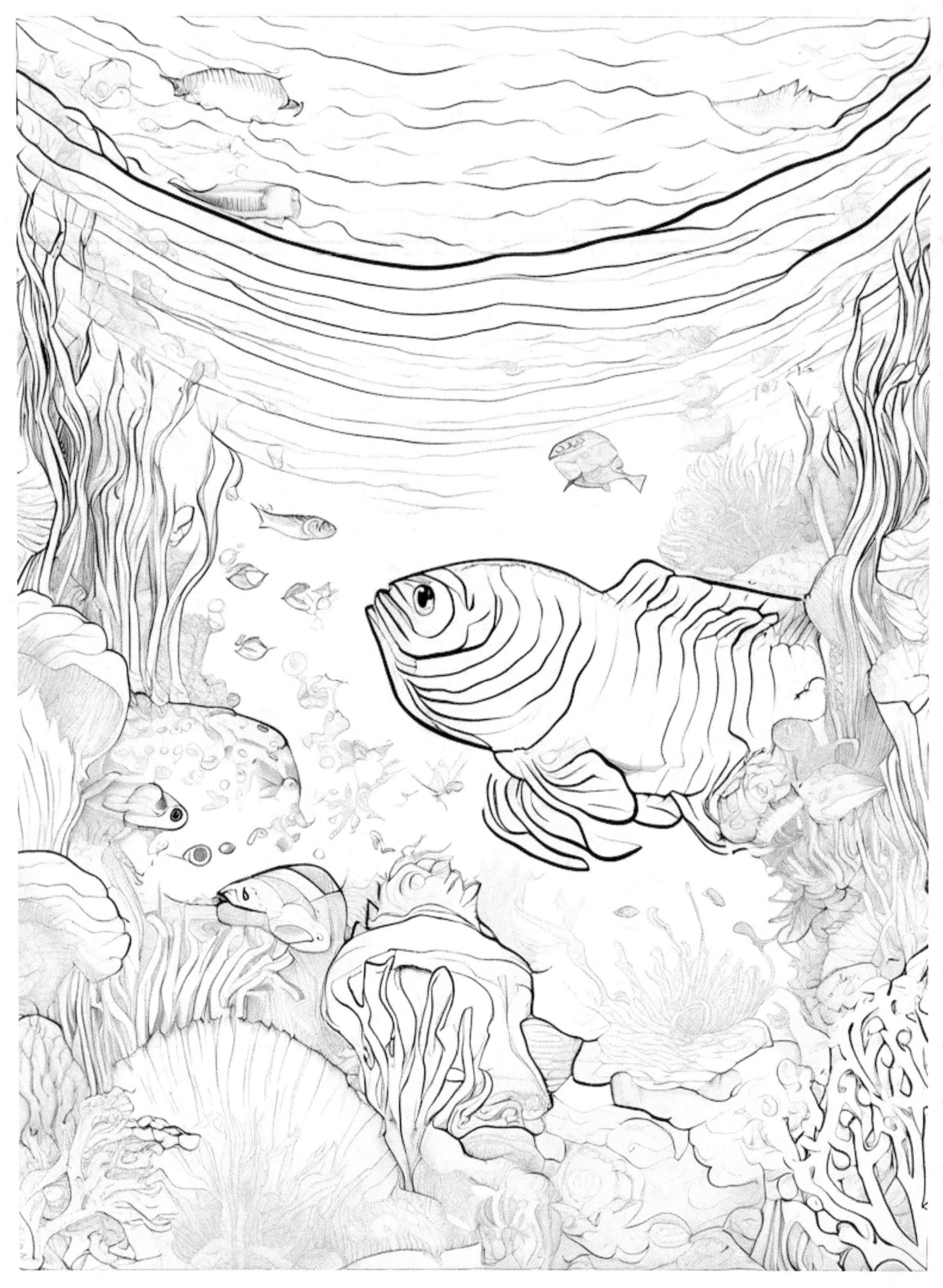

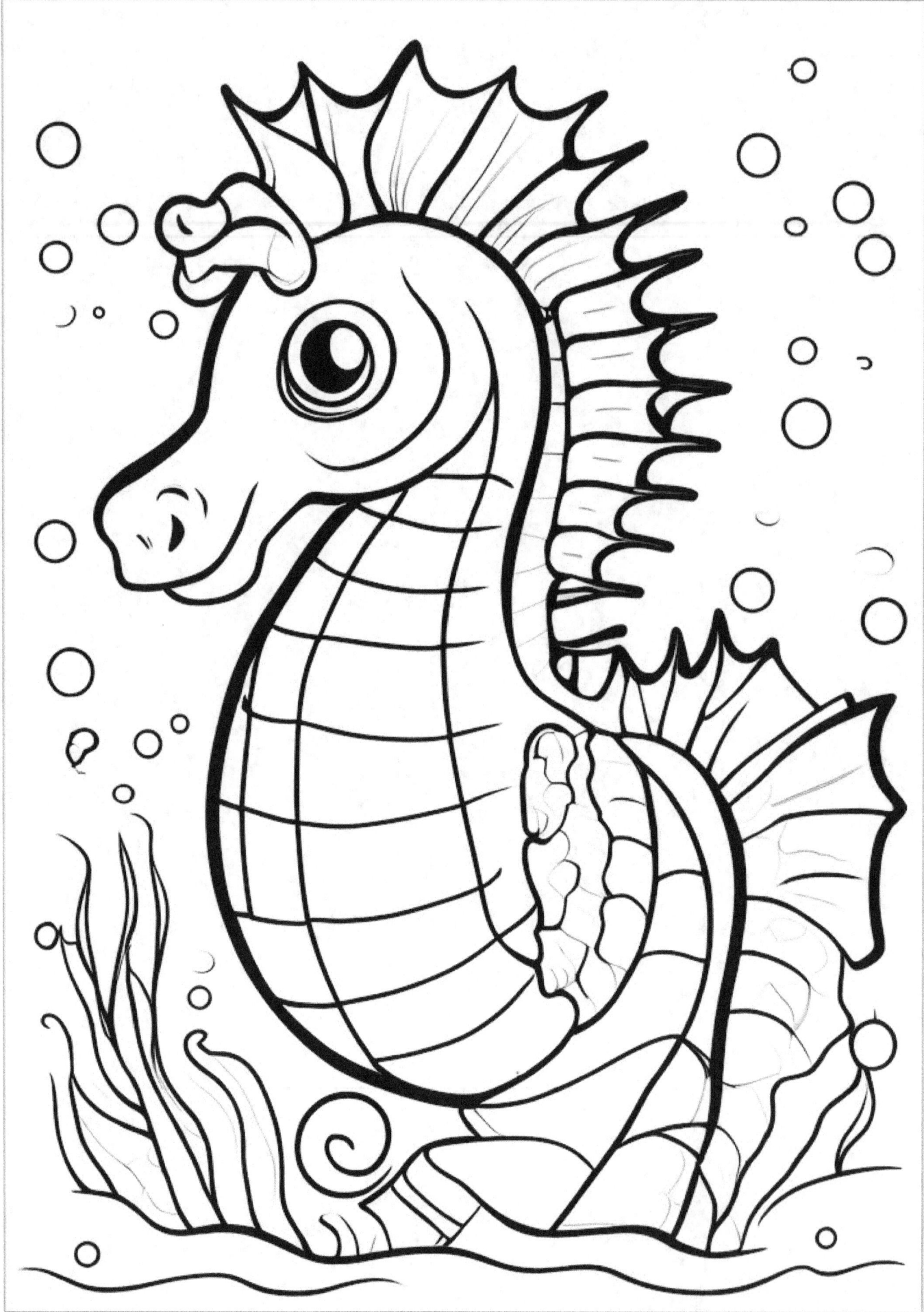

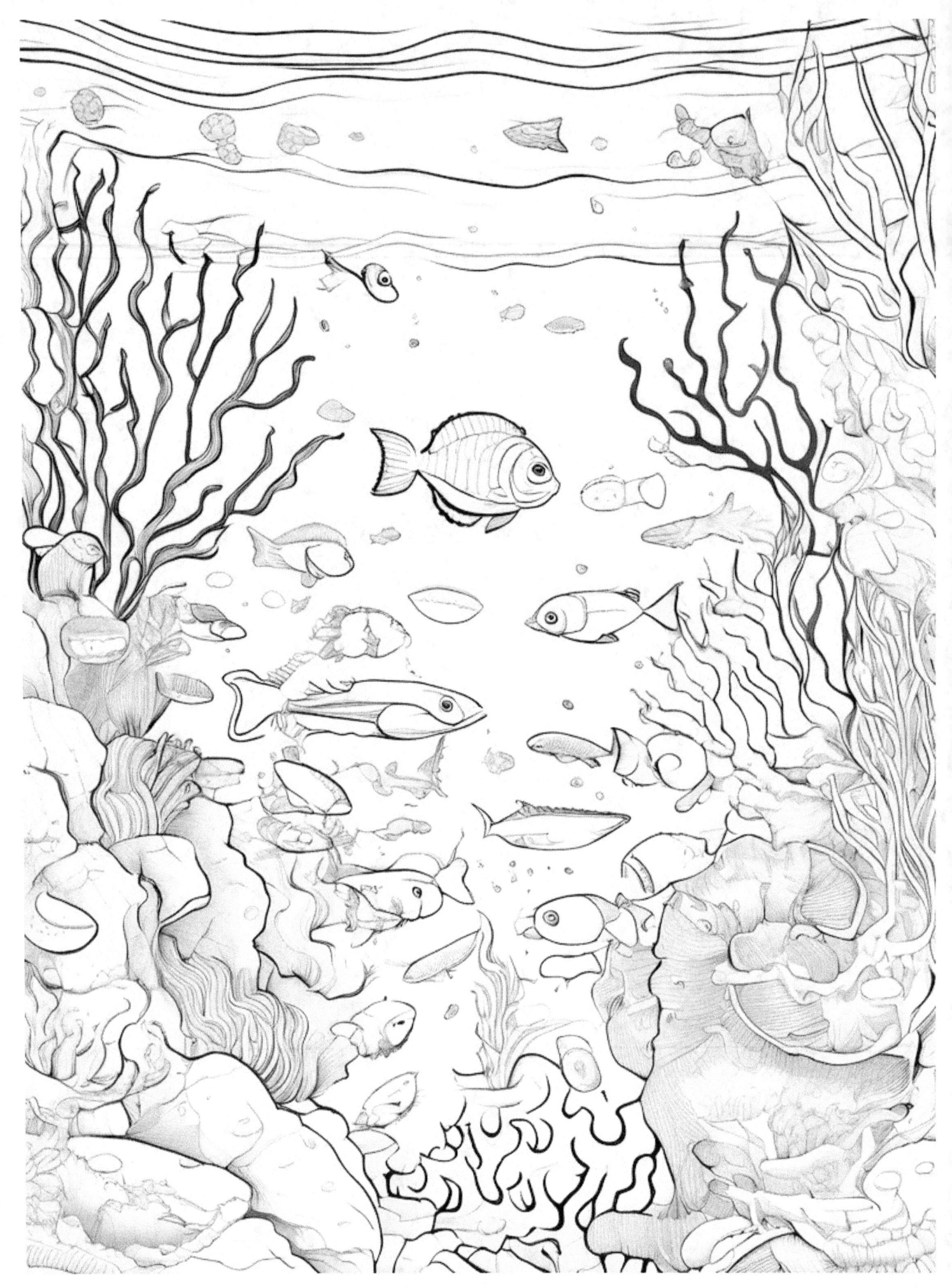

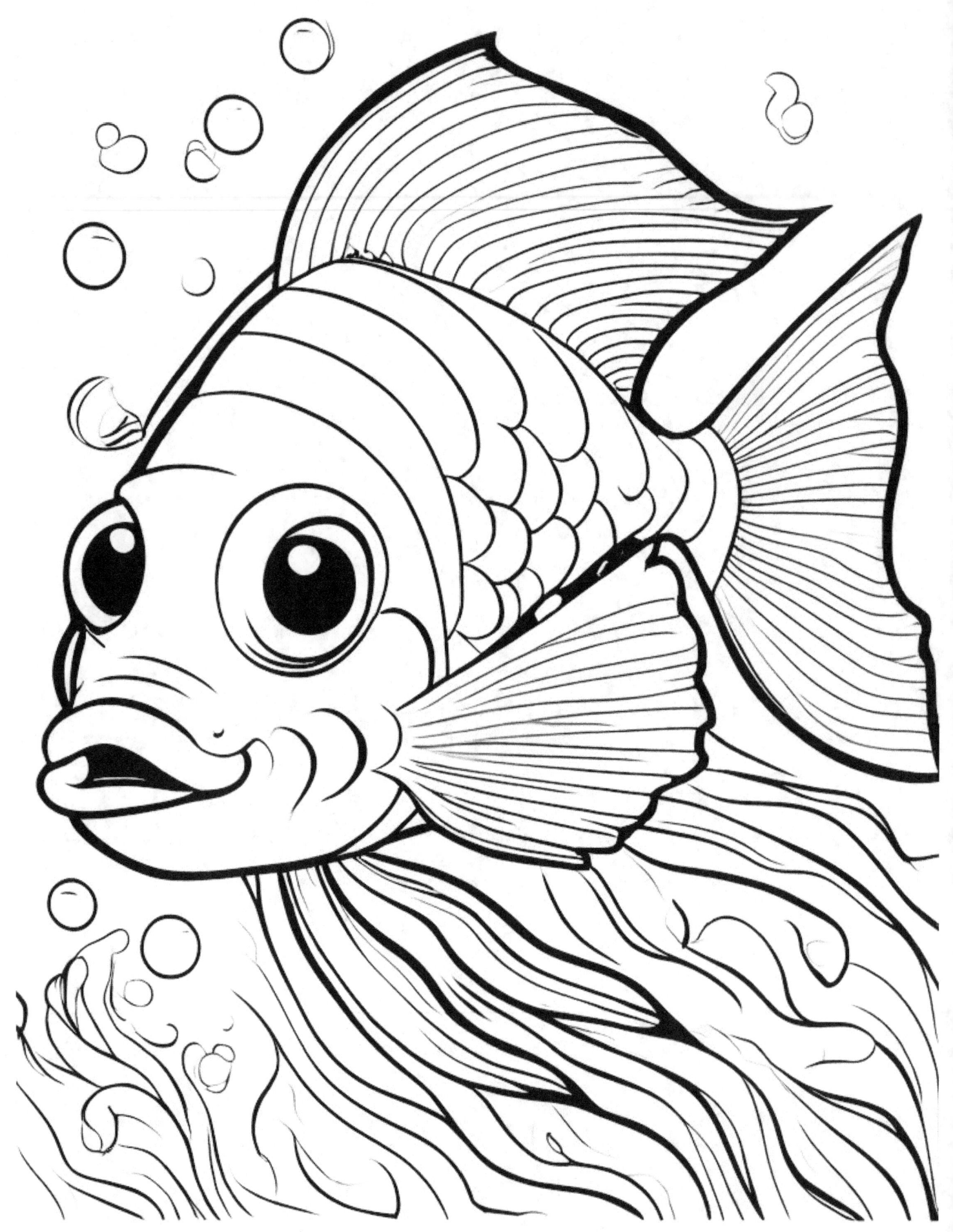

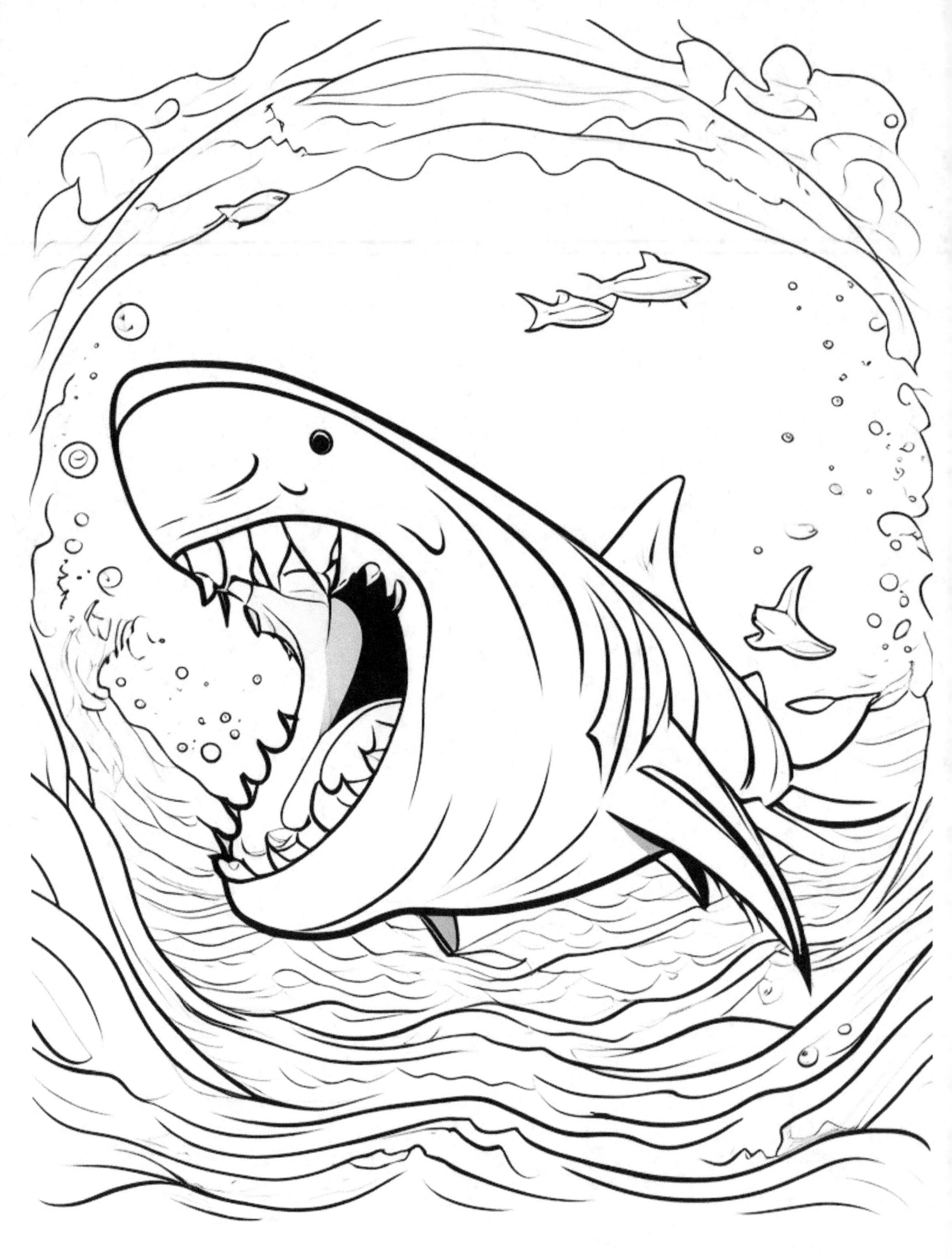

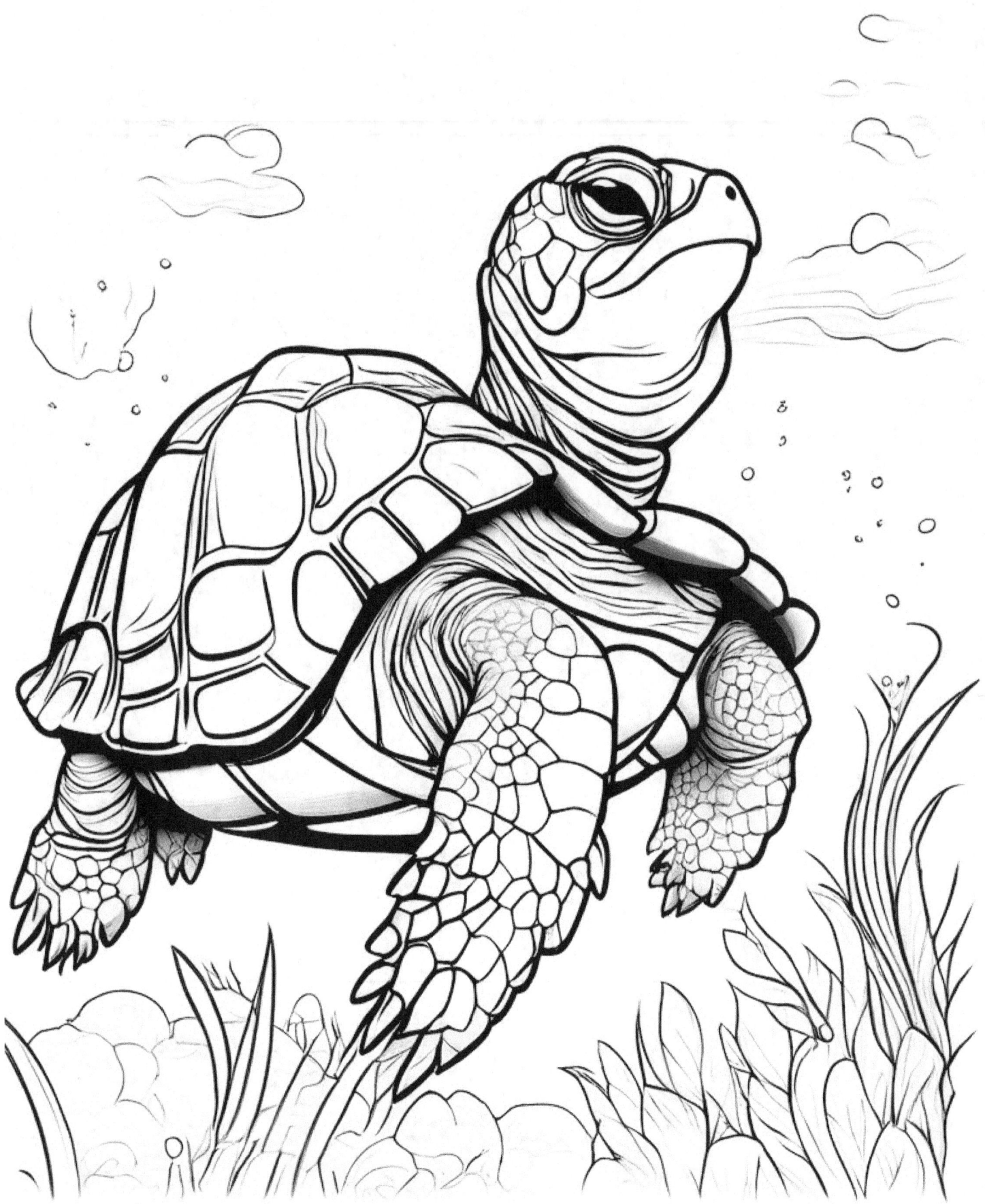

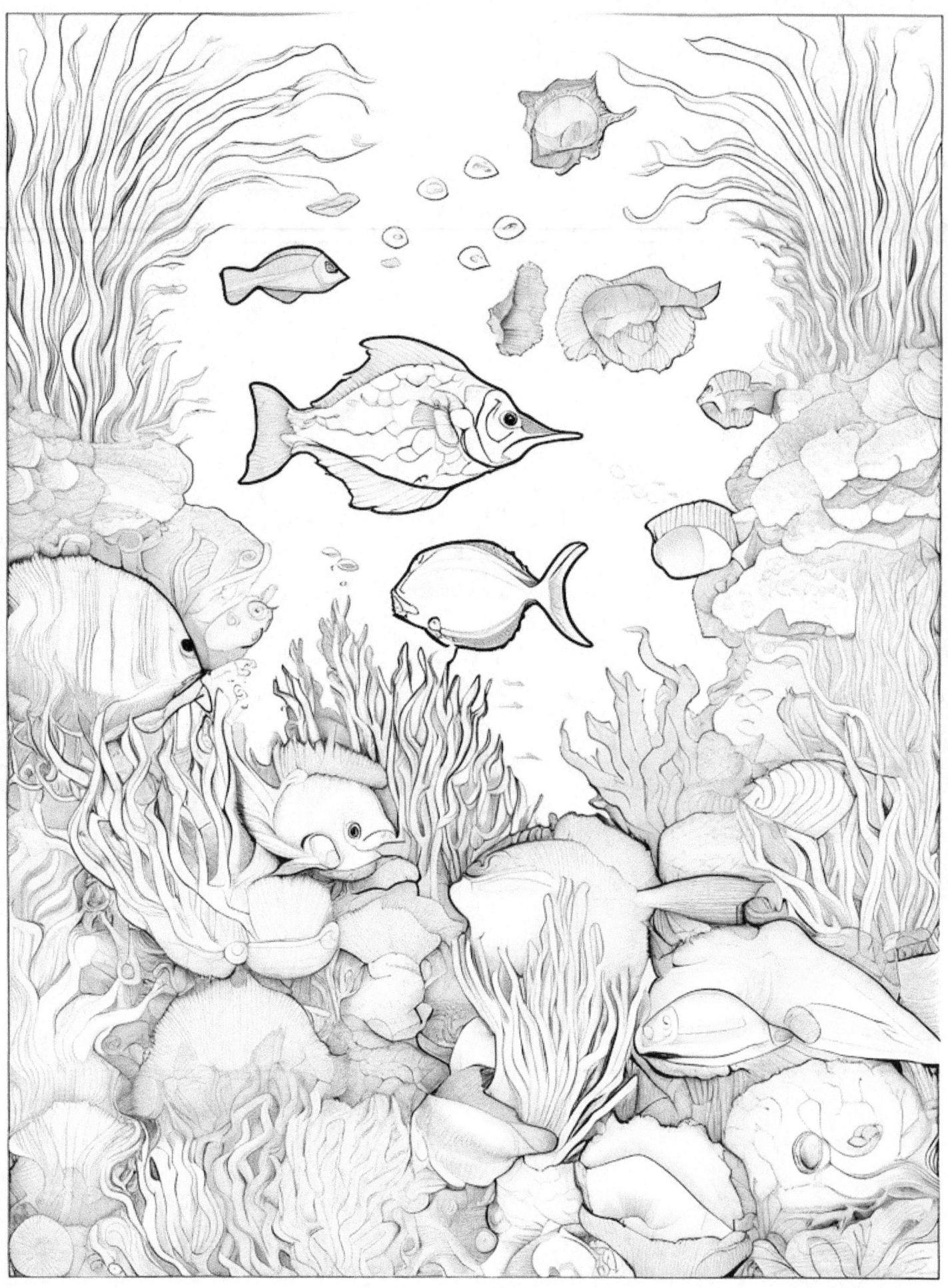

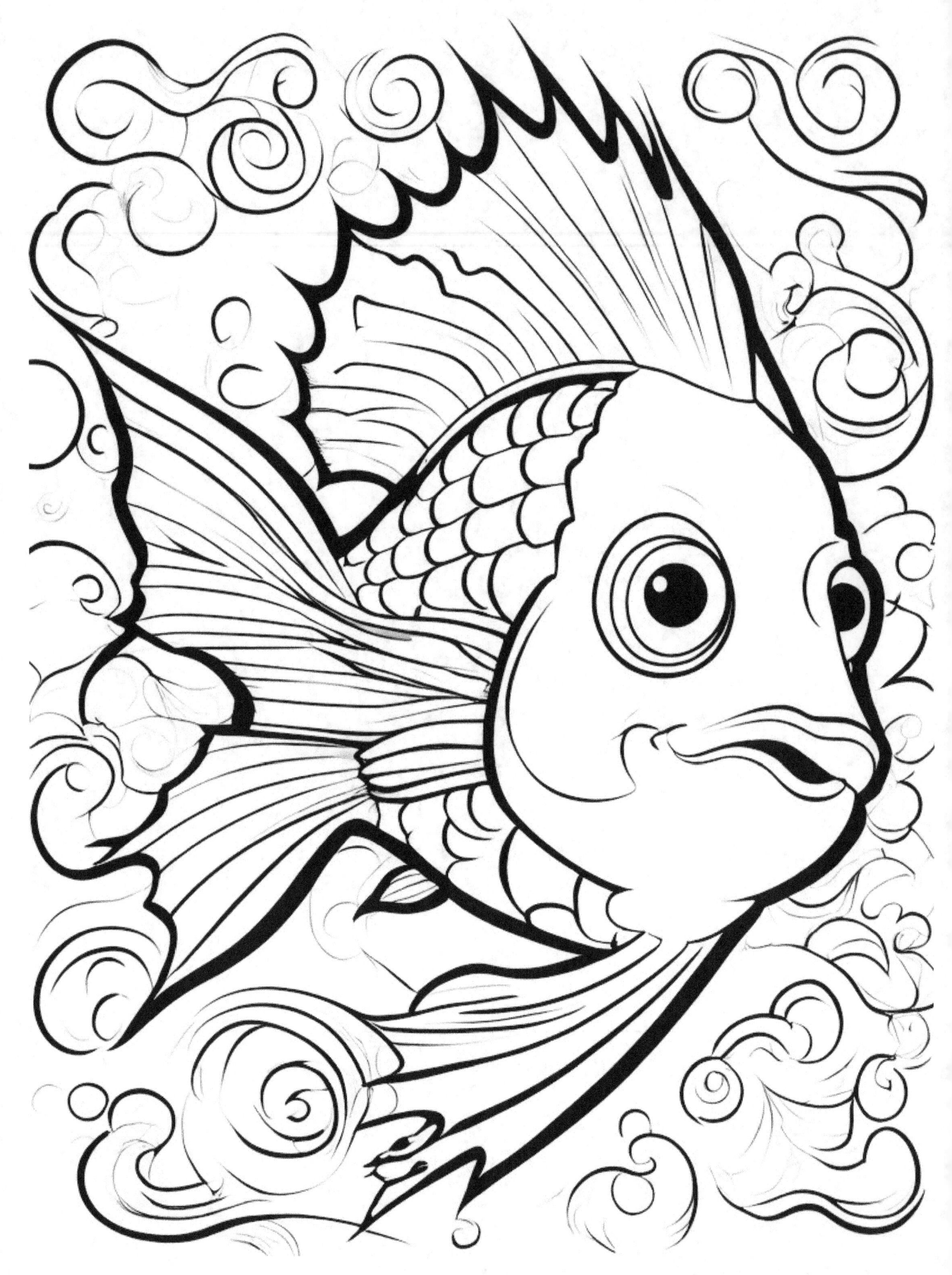

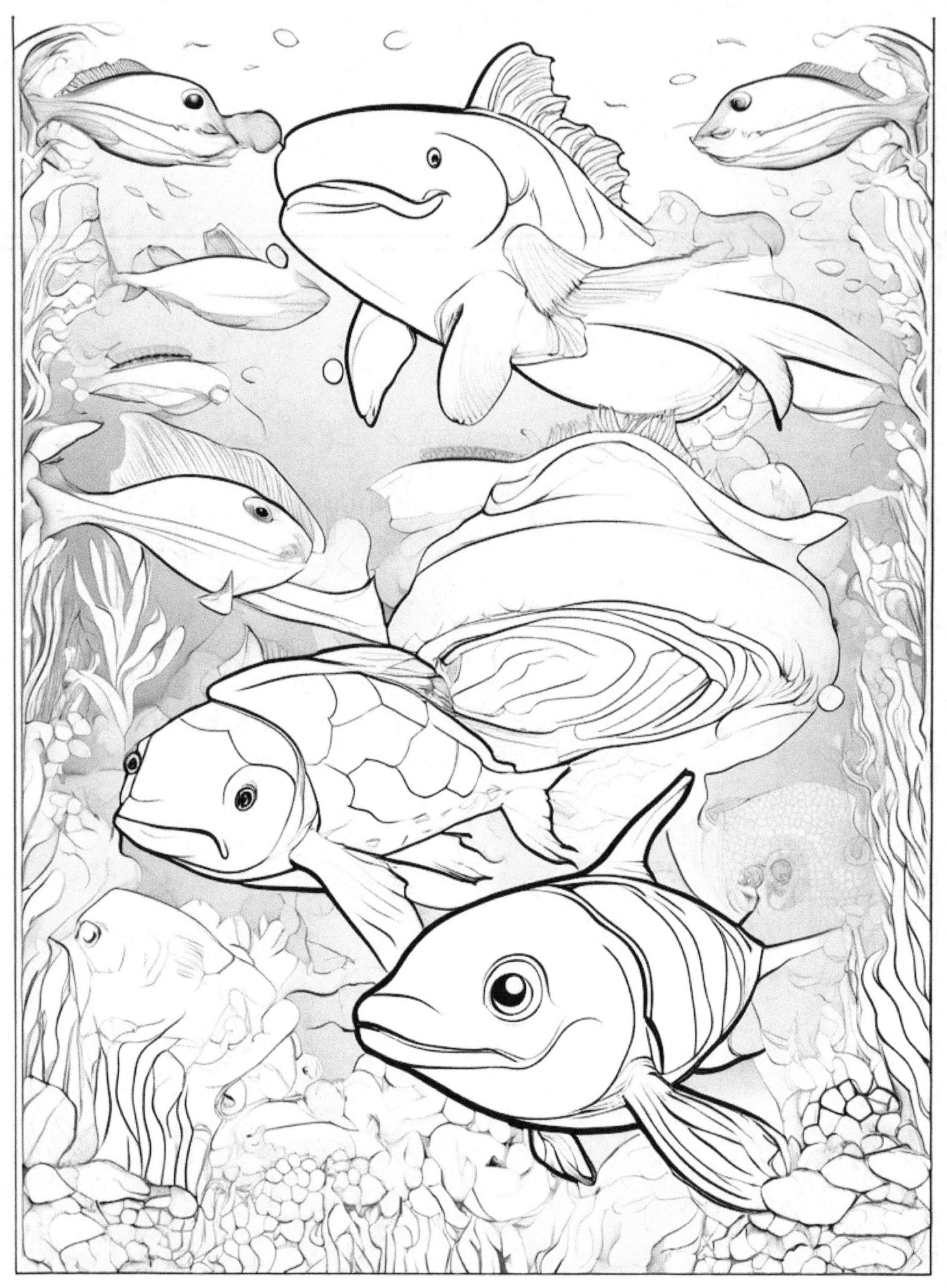

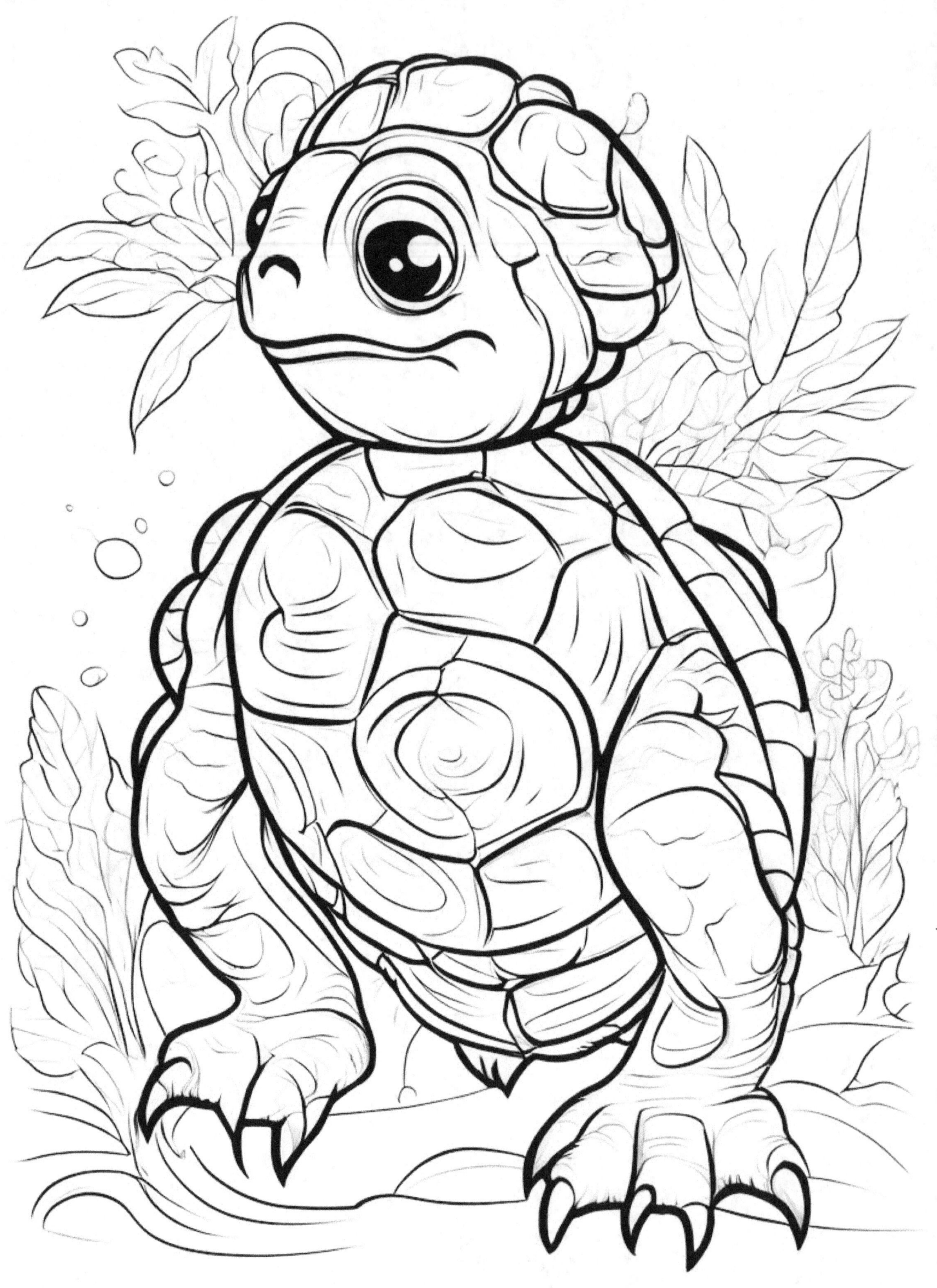

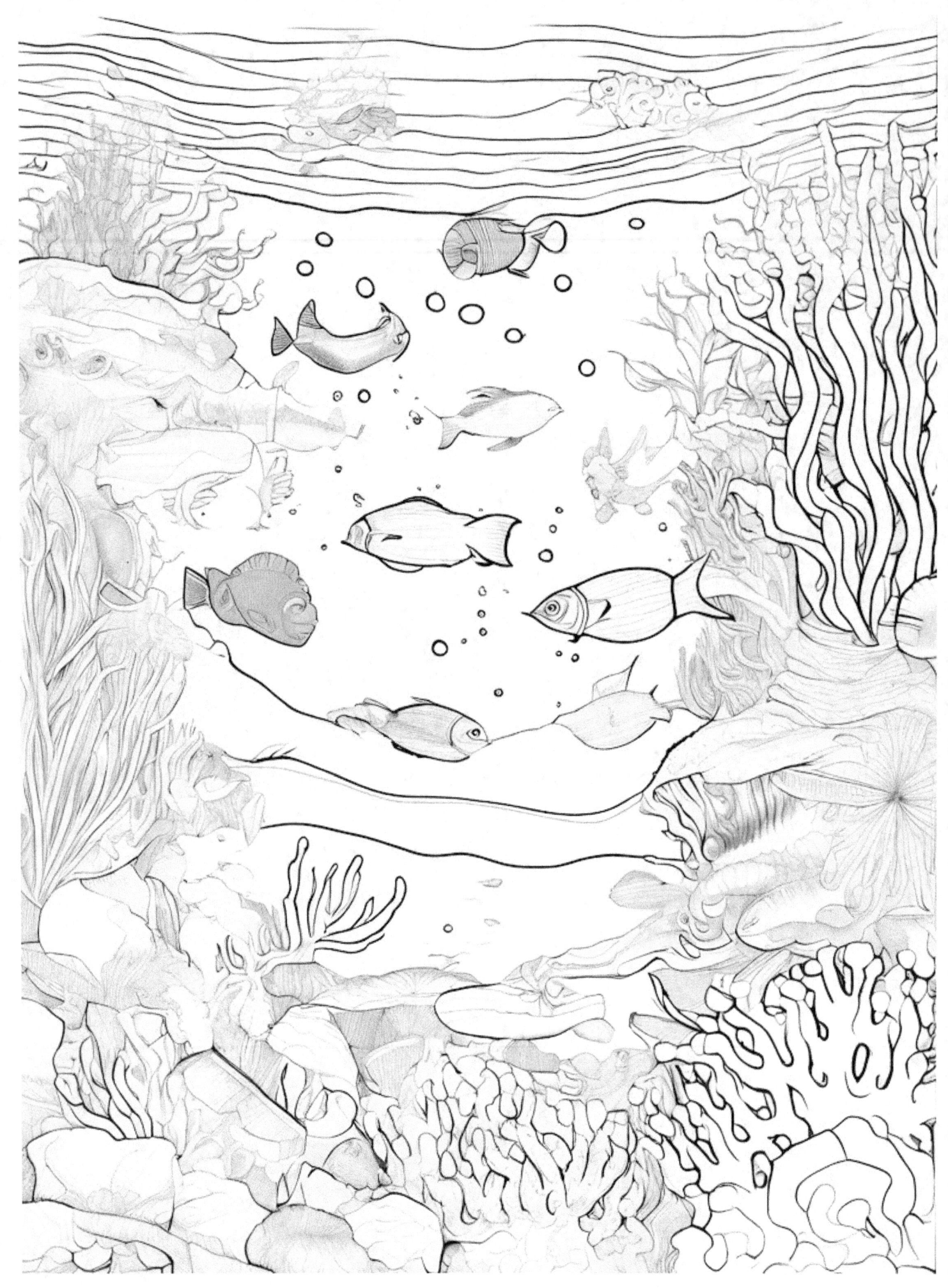

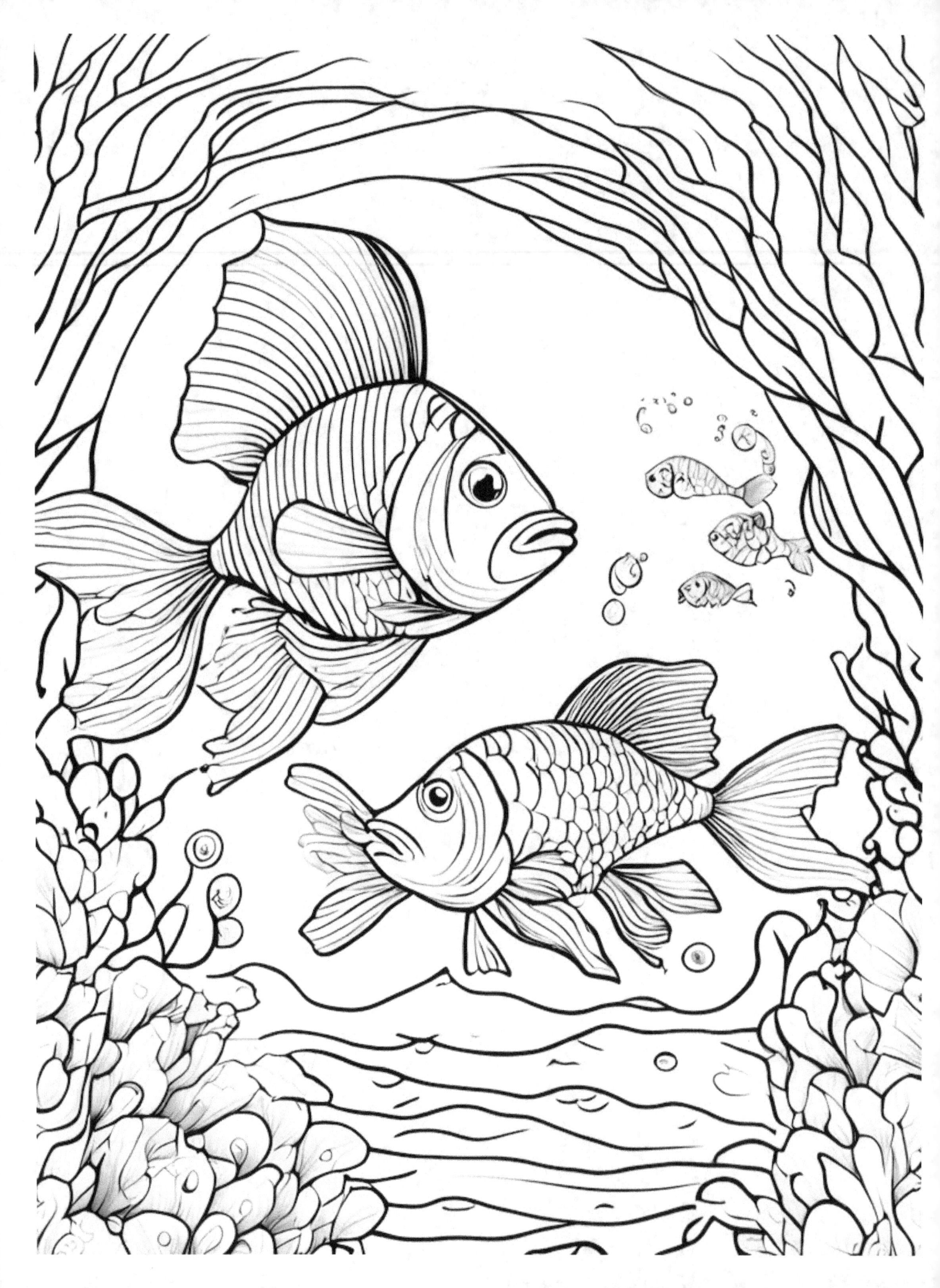

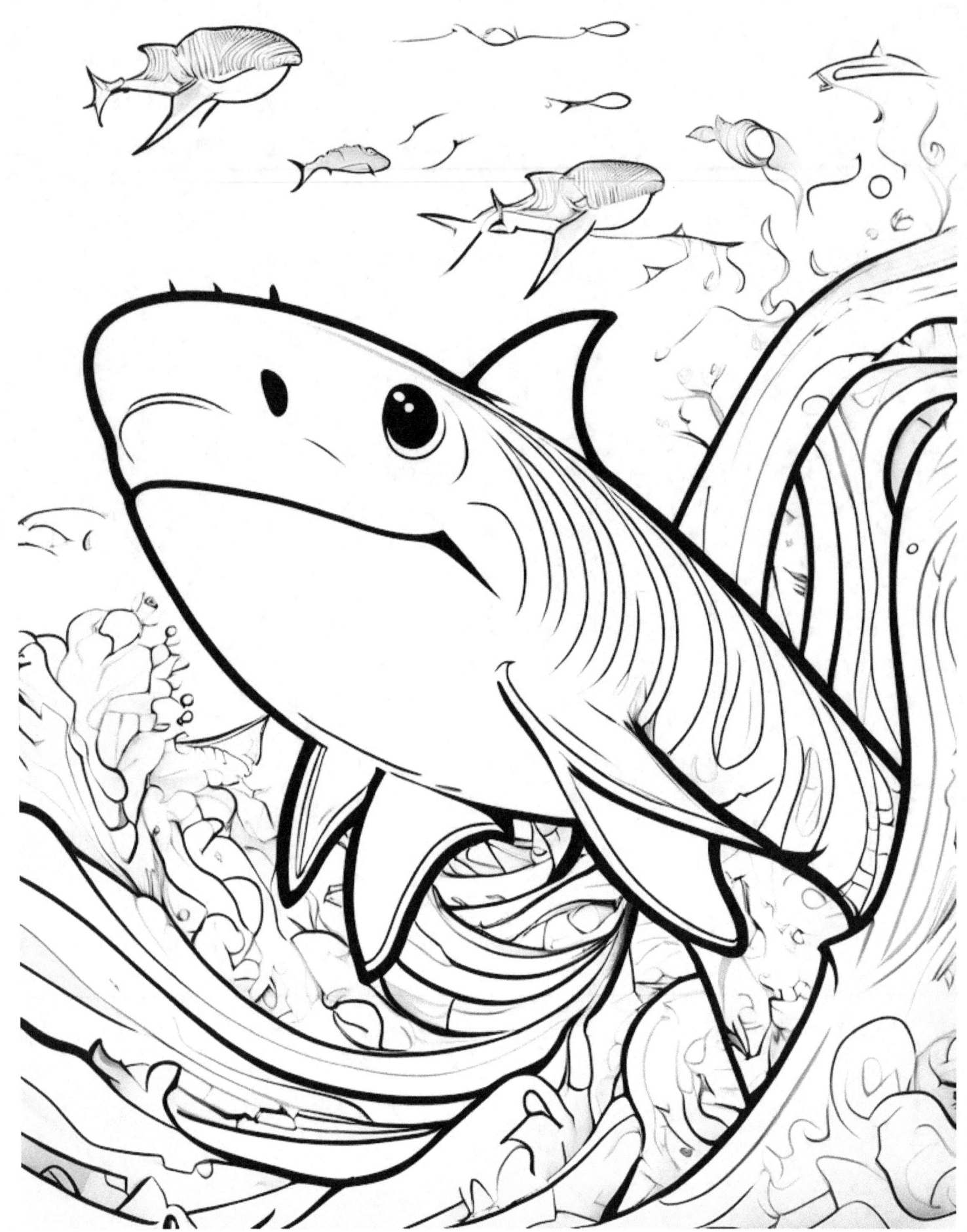

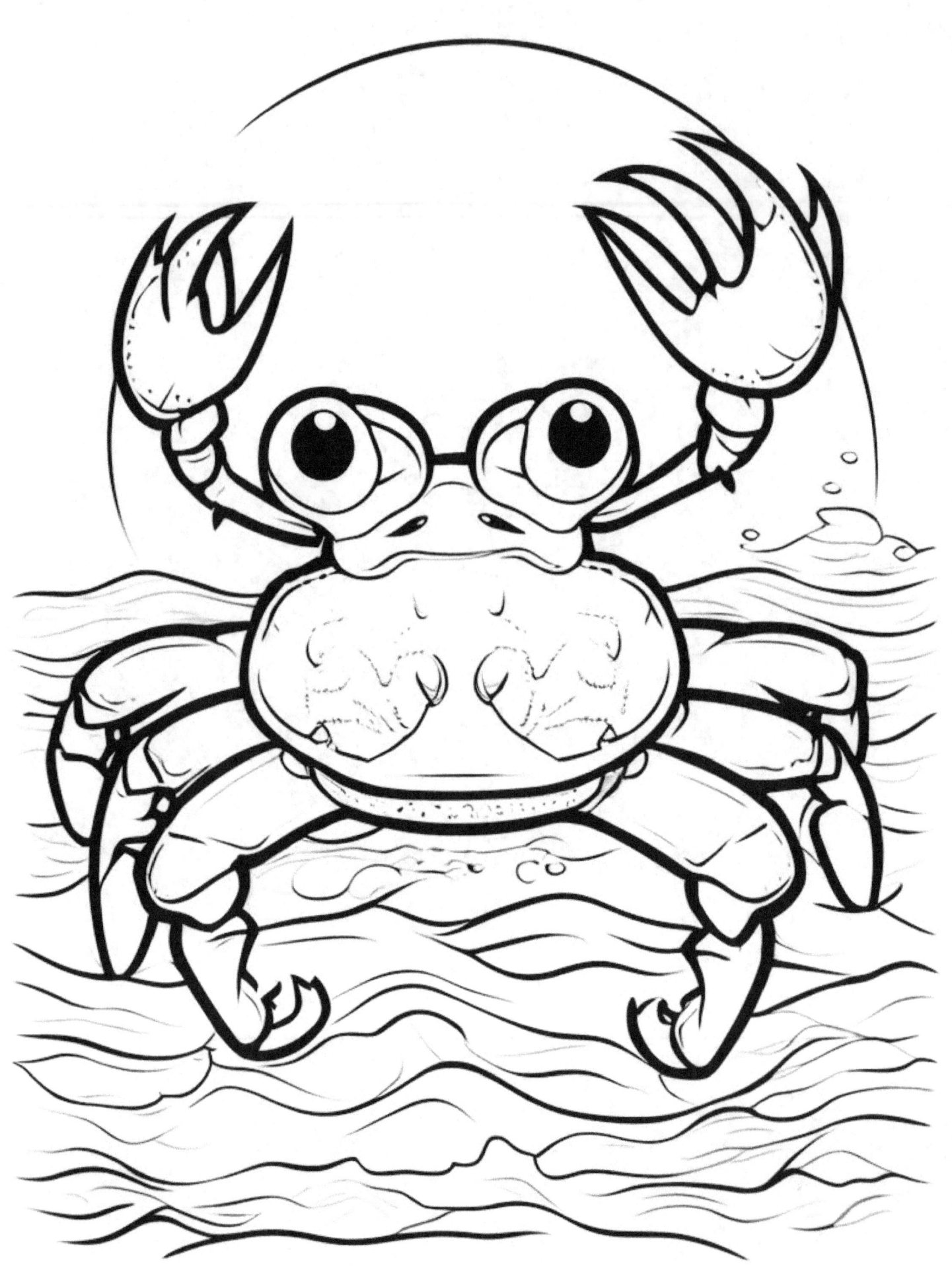

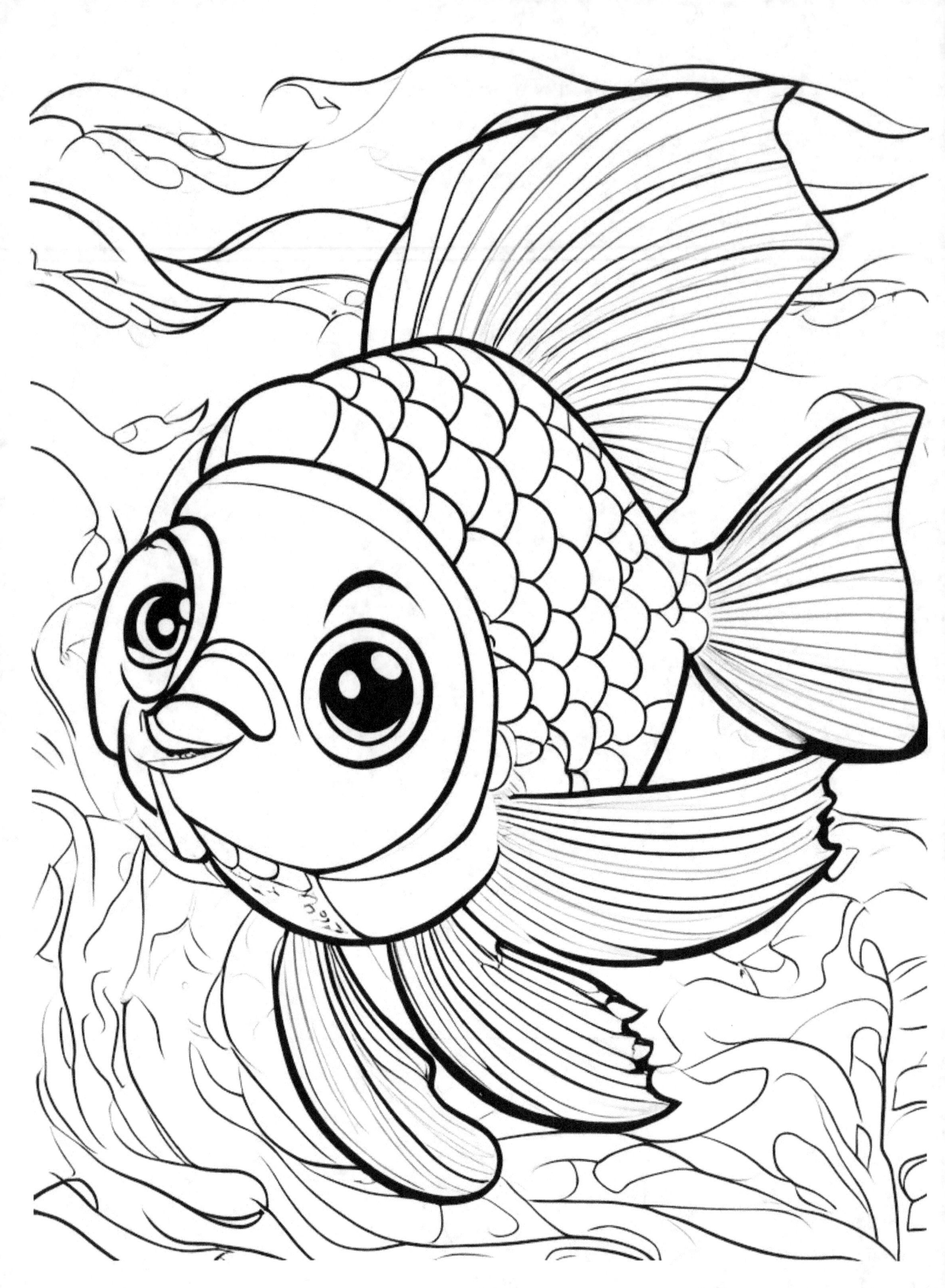

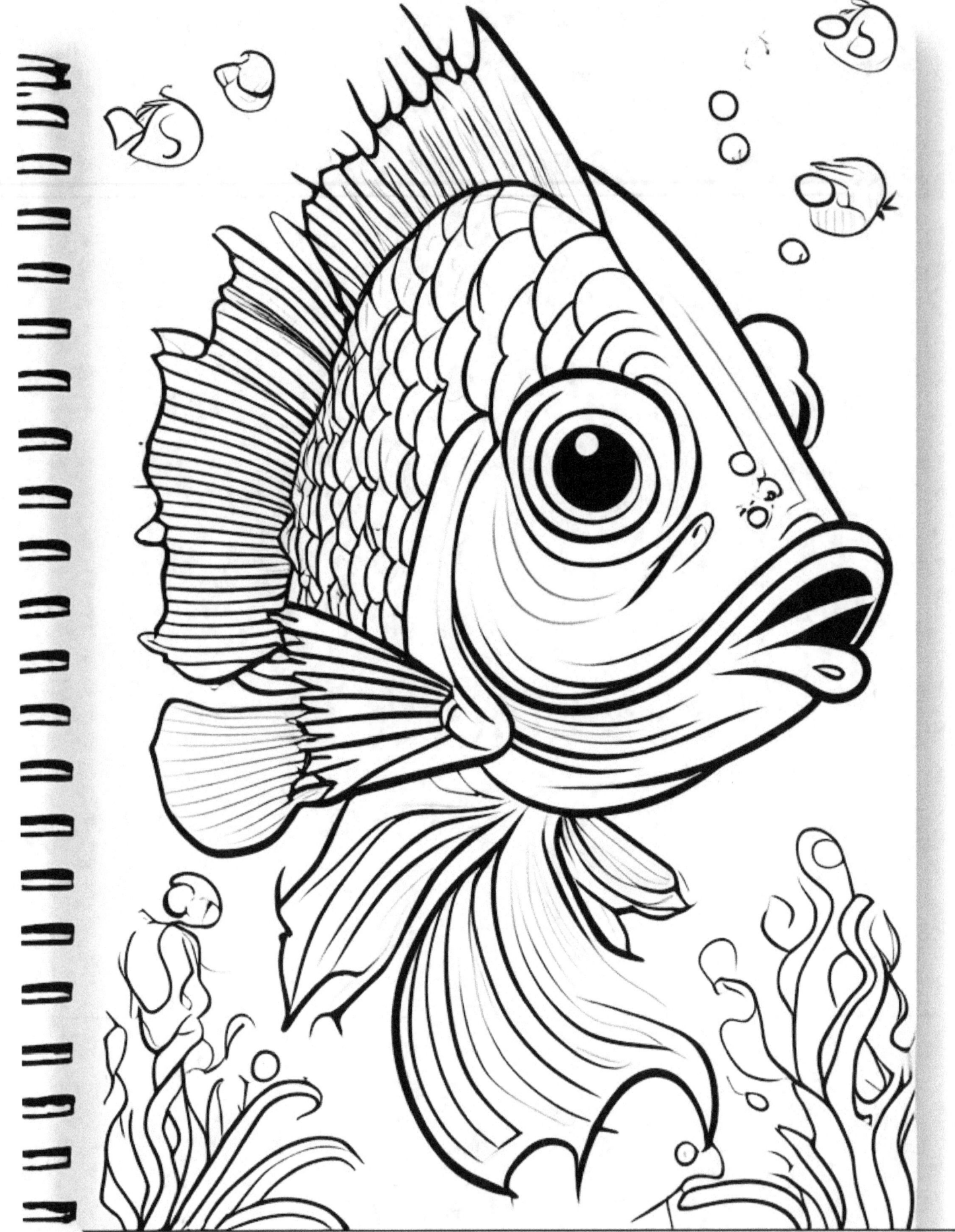